D0396531

IMAGES OF A FREE PRESS

IMAGES OF A FREE PRESS

Lee C. Bollinger

THE UNIVERSITY OF CHICAGO PRESS *Chicago & London*

Lee C. Bollinger, author of *The Tolerant Society,* is dean of the University of Michigan Law School.

Versions of parts of the following articles by Lee C. Bollinger have been used in various chapters: "Freedom of the Press and Public Access: Towards a Theory of Partial Regulation of the Mass Media," 75 Mich. L. Rev. 1 (1976), appears in Chapters 5 and 6; "On the Legal Relationship between Old and New Technologies of Communication," 26 German Yearbook of International Law 269 (1983), in Chapter 5; and "The Rationality of Public Regulation of the Media" in *Democracy and the Mass Media,* ed. Judith Lichtenberg (Cambridge: Cambridge University Press, 1990), in Chapters 6 and 7.

The University of Chicago Press, Chicago 60637
The University of Chicago Press, Ltd., London

Library of Congress Cataloging-in-Publication Data

Bollinger, Lee C., 1946–
    Images of a free press / Lee C. Bollinger.
        p.   cm.
    Includes bibliographical references and index.
    ISBN 0-226-06348-8
    1. Freedom of the press—United States. 2. Freedom of speech—United States. 3. Mass media—Law and legislation—United States.
    I. Title.
    KF4774.B65   1991
    342.73'0853—dc20
    [347.302853]   90-27740
                                                              CIP

⊗ The paper used in this publication meets the minimum requirements of the American National Standard for Information Sciences—Permanence of Paper for Printed Library Materials, ANSI Z39.48-1984.

To My Father

CONTENTS

ACKNOWLEDGMENTS

This book has had a long period of gestation, but that only means I have had more time to receive help from more people. Now, at last, it is time to thank them. My father, who was the editor and publisher of a small town newspaper while I was growing up, instilled in me early a deep respect for the calling of journalism as well as for the hard-won craft of writing well. For this, and for so much more, this book is dedicated to him. My wife, Jean, has been an inspiring and resourceful critic, respectful enough of the enterprise but skeptical enough of my execution to make her the perfect ally. Many colleagues and friends provided support and criticism throughout the years I have reflected on these issues. Of these I am especially indebted to Vincent Blasi, Robert Burt, Ronald Gilson, Steven Helle, Richard Lempert, Joseph Sax, Frederick Schauer, Steven Shiffrin, and James Boyd White. Two readers for the press (one of whom, Scot Powe, waived his anonymity) also provided very helpful suggestions.

Several students rendered valuable research assistance: Eric Barron, Nancy Borland, John Christopher, Hilda Harris, Jana Henkel, Laura Schacter, and Charles Tea. I want to thank especially Ken Wittenberg, who was tireless in trying to satisfy my requests for relevant but difficult-to-find materials.

I am also grateful for the editorial assistance of Jan Opdyke, who helped tighten the manuscript considerably, and of Lila Weinberg, senior manuscript editor at the University of Chicago Press, who was extremely patient with last-minute additions and thorough in pulling everything together into a final whole.

Finally, I wish to thank my administrative associate, Lillian Fritzler, for hard work, graciously performed, in helping to prepare the manuscript.

L.C.B.

Ann Arbor, Michigan
November 1990

INTRODUCTION

For nearly two decades I have taught courses on the subject of mass media law. During that time the subject has become a field. When I started, with a seminar, it was the only offering in that general area at the University of Michigan Law School. That was not atypical for law schools. To be sure, some of the material that would eventually compose a mass media law course was covered in other courses at the time: the First Amendment component of the basic course in constitutional law included at least some of the press cases, and first-year torts professors would sometimes find their way to areas of defamation and invasion of privacy. But these were just parts of other fields. There was no casebook to speak of.

Today, mass media law courses are regularly included in the curricula of law schools throughout the country. There are all the indicia of a field: several casebooks by prominent legal academics; a looseleaf, up-to-date, reporter series specifically called the Media Law Reporter; and a substantial and complex literature by experts. The field was born sometime around 1980.

Over the years I have written several articles that bear directly on the themes of this book. Many of the ideas developed in those articles are woven together here. But the final overview is new. The earlier work, while informing the general perspective now taken, is preparatory.

I have written this book with a diverse audience in mind, hoping to provide a primer, a basic overview, of the law regarding freedom of the press for those who do not have any special knowledge of it. This is not, however, a treatise. It is not intended to be, nor, fortuitously, has it turned out to be, a comprehensive description of the cases or the laws governing the press, its freedom, and its obligations. Rather, it is an interpretive enterprise, cast in the mold of a series of reflections. As such, it is selective in what it includes, though not, I believe, at the cost of distorting reality.

I hope this work also has relevance for those sophisticated in the field, for the reflections converge to form an approach to the concept of freedom of the press that differs from the official course now followed by the courts and generally advocated by its commentators. It is my hope that this book will serve to enlarge our vision of the idea of freedom of the press—a matter I shall address beginning in Chapter 3.

A few more warnings and disclosures are in order. First, this book is largely, though not entirely, concerned with the Supreme Court and the development of the concept of freedom of the press. Lower court and administrative cases figure importantly but not prominently. Second, insofar as this study attempts to examine the national experience with the principle of freedom of the press, it does so only for this century and only beginning with the 1920s. It is not a historical account beyond that. Third, I have not provided comprehensive references to the now myriad articles and books that compose the field. I have, of course, followed the principle of attributing ideas to their sources, but not every relevant discussion in the surrounding literature is referred to.

In the end, what is offered here is the story of mass media law as I have witnessed its composition over nearly two decades. To my mind it is an intriguing, even exciting, story. Never once have I tired of teaching it. I hope my deep affection for the subject is manifest.

The Central Image

Consider the central image of the American ideal of freedom of the press. If you were asked to explain the meaning of the principle of freedom of the press in American society, and how it works, what would you say?

I think the answer would be something like the following: In the United States the government is forbidden by virtue of the First Amendment from censoring or punishing the press for what it chooses to say. The press is not licensed, as it was in seventeenth-century England. It need not clear with the government what it proposes to publish. And, except under very limited circumstances, the government may not punish the press for what it has said. Libel, invasions of privacy, extraordinary threats to national security, and a few other justifications may permit government to limit press freedom, but these circumstances are limited and scrutinized closely by the courts. It is, indeed, the function of the courts to protect press freedom against government interference and to decide when those rare instances arise.

The principal justification for this manner of organizing society is the necessity of a free press in a democratic political system. Without it the public cannot receive all the information it needs—about government actions or public issues—to exercise its sovereign powers.

This is, roughly, the central image.

In this book, I am interested in exploring the extent to which reality differs from this initially articulated notion of what the world is like, as well as in asking whether the discrepancy (to the extent one exists) ought to be regarded as important. In one sense, the analysis is an attempt to unfold the layers of meaning we have constructed around the notion of freedom of the press. We will begin with what I think is the first layer—with the central image.

I

For the modern era, the fullest, richest articulation of the central image of freedom of the press is to be found in the Supreme Court's 1964 decision in *New York Times Co. v. Sullivan*.[1] No Supreme Court case of this century is more important to our notion of what press freedom means. It was one of those rare decisions that provided a conceptual framework and an idiom for its time. Because the Court's decision was such a formative event in the history of First Amendment treatment of the press, it is worth spending a few moments exploring it in detail.

Sullivan arose out of the struggle against segregation in the 1960s. On March 29, 1960, the New York Times had carried a full-page advertisement, signed by various clergy and civil rights activists, that charged the Montgomery, Alabama, police with conducting a "wave of terror" against Martin Luther King and others engaged in nonviolent demonstrations. The third and sixth paragraphs of the advertisement provided the grist for the libel claim:

> In Montgomery, Alabama, after students sang "My Country, 'Tis of Thee" on the State Capitol steps, their leaders were expelled from school, and truckloads of police armed with shotguns and tear-gas ringed the Alabama State College Campus. When the entire student body protested to state authorities by refusing to re-register, their dining hall was padlocked in an attempt to starve them into submission.
>
> Again and again the Southern violators have answered Dr. King's peaceful protests with intimidation and violence. They have bombed his home almost killing his wife and child. They have assaulted his person. They have arrested him seven times—for "speeding," "loitering" and

similar "offenses." And now they have charged him with "perjury"—a *felony* under which they could imprison him for *ten years*.[2]

L. B. Sullivan was an elected commissioner of Montgomery, whose responsibilities included oversight of the local police department. Though unnamed in the advertisement, he claimed that these paragraphs libeled him because readers would assume that he was responsible for the acts they alleged: that the police had attempted to "starve" the student protestors, had arrested Dr. King on trumped-up charges, had assaulted him, bombed his home, and falsely charged him with a crime.

The New York Times and its codefendants, four individuals whose names had appeared as sponsors (who, incidentally, denied having authorized the use of their names), conceded that the advertisement contained several errors. These ranged from the trivial to the potentially significant. Students had demanded service at a segregated lunch counter at the county courthouse, and nine of them had been expelled. When protesting at the state capitol, they sang "The Star Spangled Banner," not "My Country, 'Tis of Thee." Finally, Martin Luther King had been arrested not seven but four times, and the assault was contested.

Under Alabama libel law, Sullivan was able to put the statements of the advertisement into evidence, assert that they were false, claim that the average reader would assume he was responsible for the acts charged, and rest his case.[3] Because the statements concerned his occupation, Sullivan did not have to submit evidence that his reputation had actually been diminished by the statements (these constituted "libel per se"). All he had to do was call witnesses who would testify that they had read the article and assumed it referred to him—or, in legal terminology, assumed that the defamatory statements were "of and concerning" him. This, of course, he did. Then he asked for damages of $500,000, to compensate him for the injury to his reputation and to punish the defendants for having caused it. (In other words, he requested compensation for both "general" and "punitive" damages.)

The New York Times could escape liability, primarily by either establishing that the statements were true or by showing that, even if false, they were not "of and concerning" the plaintiff.

The trial judge submitted the evidence to the jury, with the instructions that general damages were to be presumed, since the statement constituted libel per se, and that the jury had only to determine whether the statements were made "of and concerning" the plaintiff. Then it could proceed to ascertain the amount of compensation, with the caveat that punitive damages required an additional finding that the New York Times, and other defendants, had been more than "careless." The jury returned a verdict for $500,000.

New York Times v. Sullivan came to the Supreme Court with high drama. The result of this particular case—a $500,000 verdict against the Times—was startling. The newspaper's attorneys told the Court that four additional lawsuits based on the advertisement had been brought, with alleged damages totaling $2,500,000.[4] The case raised an important general First Amendment issue also: the question whether the common law action for libel would be subjected to the strictures of the First Amendment. Because Alabama's libel law was similar to those of many states, it was an appropriate test case. Two decades earlier the Court had ruled that libel was an area of speech regulation untouched by the First Amendment.[5] A major question was whether the Court would continue to stand by that position.

Beyond the legal issues in the case, the dispute was inescapably infused with the aura and symbolism of the great desegregation conflict. Only the most dull-minded could have been insensible to the North-South dimension of the case, or have missed the role chance suddenly provided for this otherwise modest civil action for libel to serve as a foot soldier in the larger social struggle. The Supreme Court itself was hardly a bystander in that struggle; it had been its principal incipient. And there was no doubt where the New York Times was aligned in the conflict.

All of these radiant significances were there to be observed, but, when *New York Times v. Sullivan* reached the Supreme Court, few might have guessed that the greatest significance of the occasion would be for the First Amendment as a whole. For *New York Times v. Sullivan* was not to become merely a holding about libel law and the First Amendment, nor yet another battlefield in the modern civil war over segregation. In the end it provided a major modern context for defining the underlying meaning of the First Amendment.

The Court's opinion, written by Justice Brennan, posed the issue to be faced in such a way that a major theoretical inquiry was required. At issue was the scope of First Amendment protection to be afforded "citizens" speaking out on the issues of the day who, in the course of so doing, criticize "government officials." To address that issue the Court had to provide theories and characterizations about some profound matters: about the desirability of open public debate among citizens; about the effects on citizens of a law that made false statements of fact actionable (which in turn necessitated an understanding of the psychology of citizens, of the psychology of government officials who might base lawsuits on such a law, and of the capacity of the legal system to separate good from bad claims); and, finally, about the nature of the competing interests that would be sacrificed by a decision to expand the range of protected citizen commentary.

To the questions posed by these issues the Court gave the following answers. The value of freedom of speech and press is that it supports the societal choice for a democratic system of government. In that political scheme, the people are the true and final sovereign, the government at any given time merely their representative. The Court spoke admiringly, and in James Madison's words, of the role of the "citizen-critic" and of how "the censorial power is in the people over the Government, and not in the Government over the people."[6]

Under such an arrangement, however, government is frequently unhappy, for it is always inclined to preserve and extend its powers by limiting the speech that threatens it. An attempt of that sort succeeded in 1798, when Congress enacted the Sedition Act, making it a crime to criticize the government with improper motives and so bring it into disrepute.[7] This law struck at the heart of the democracy because it prevented citizens from participating in public life while enhancing the ability of the existing state to wield unreviewable power. It was, psychologically, the equivalent of a child usurping the role of the parent.

The Court in 1964 described it as the sad episode in American history that "first crystallized a national awareness of the central meaning of the First Amendment."[8]

Thus, in its ruling on *New York Times v. Sullivan*, the Court pronounced both the existence and the location of the "central" image of freedom of speech and press. It was an image of essential violation of the minimal conditions demanded by democratic principles. For speech and press freedom, it provided the starting point.

From this core meaning the Court thought it could divine answers to such spiraling questions as the specific one before it in *Sullivan*: libel drew the line at falsehood, but that was too close to First Amendment bone because even falsehoods have value in public debate, producing, in the words of John Stuart Mill, "the clearer perception and livelier impression of truth, produced by its collision with error."[9] Furthermore, the system cannot afford to banish falsehoods from public debate, even if they are valueless, for at the same time it would inevitably excise much that was true and good. And it must be acknowledged that the legal system, which is called upon to draw these crucial distinctions, is imperfectly equipped for the task. Not every truthful claim triumphs in the marketplace of the trial. Evidence is sometimes hard to come by, and too expensive to produce in court when it is. To err is human, and the legal system is human. And, given the American rule that the costs of litigation are borne by each party, every victory has its price and that price is itself a kind of fine.

Along with its self-portrait of the legal system, the Court offered a psychological portrait of the citizenry, and, by extension, the press. It was a contradictory depiction, though the contradiction was left unnoted. On one hand, *Sullivan* portrayed the citizen as reluctant to enter public debate, timid before the prospect of a lawsuit, fearful of the costs. One naturally imagines a citizenry composed of people with other things to do, who see participation in public affairs as a duty, not a joy, as something to be avoided when an excuse is at hand.

Yet *Sullivan* also provides the image of a citizen who is naturally disposed to enter public debate—in fact, too disposed. Believing deeply and finding opposing beliefs threatening, this person is inclined to resort to "exaggeration, to vilification . . . and even to false statement."[10] Public discussion is not a pretty thing because belief pushes people to adversarial extremes and citizens cannot control themselves.

Contradictory though this portrait may be, it led the Court to a single conclusion. The fact that people are reluctant participants in public discussion requires us to arrange matters so that there is plenty of "breathing space" for erroneous statements. Citizens must know that a mistake will not bring verdicts hurling down upon their heads. But, the human tendency to speak uncontrollably also requires an arrangement under which people have room to err without legal consequence. Here the logic of the argument is less clear, but the idea seems to be that it is a serious mistake for the law to try to forbid something that nearly everyone is inclined to do and that people will be unable to control even if it is demanded of them. Persons who do these undesirable things are not "morally culpable," said the Court, again quoting Mill.[11] Under the circumstances, libel law has the futility and injustice of punishing that which it is only human to do.

Against these considerations the Court had to place the state's interest in limiting defamatory speech. That interest was said to lie in protecting individual reputation, presumably the pain and pecuniary injury suffered when reputation is tarnished through falsehood. Clearly, this is not an insignificant issue, but the Court found it outweighed by the public interest in (using words that were to become famous) "uninhibited, robust, and wide-open" debate.[12]

The Supreme Court in *New York Times v. Sullivan* saw in this particular application of the common law of libel by the Alabama courts a deep and profound issue of political relationships implicated, and refracted, through the First Amendment. And so the Court built a theory of the political system and a psychological theory of its members—the state, the press, and the people. In doing so it also defined a role for itself.

Professor Harry Kalven was the leading First Amendment scholar of his generation, and in the year following the *Sullivan* decision he published an article applauding and remarking upon its stunning significance. He praised the Court for initiating development of a working psychology of the general citizenry and the legal system.[13] But he also saw *Sullivan* as seminal because with it the Court embarked on a journey that would lead it to protect all speech needed for authentic public debate. "The closing question," Kalven concluded, "is whether the treatment of seditious libel as the key concept for development of appropriate constitutional doctrine will prove germinal." Though he thought it "not easy to predict what the Court will see in the Times opinion as the years roll by," because the Court "may regard the opinion as covering simply one pocket of cases, those dealing with libel of public officials, and not destructive of the earlier notions that are inconsistent only with the larger reading of the Court's action," to Kalven "the invitation to follow a dialectic progression from public official to government policy to public policy to matters in the public domain, like art," seemed "overwhelming."[14] After *Sullivan,* the task ahead was to clear away the legal brush hampering the free passage of information and ideas to the public.

II

As the years have rolled by, the Court has indeed seen *New York Times v. Sullivan* as a fountainhead. A survey of its principal decisions will convey the strength and nature of this steady refinement of the free press concept—and provide a background for the discussion in succeeding chapters.

Libel

By now there is an elaborate regime of cases, and an equally elaborate set of rules, which control the impact of libel law on public debate about public issues. Kalven's fear that the impact of *Sullivan* might be limited to cases involving public officials was, in retrospect, unwarranted. In the early 1970s a plurality of the Court was prepared to extend *Sullivan* to apply to all discussion of public issues, so that the citizen who defamed anyone in the course of public debate could not be sued for libel unless he or she had spoken defamatory falsehoods knowingly or in reckless disregard of the truth.[15] But a majority of the Court never formed around this idea. Instead, it settled on a position that continued *Sullivan's* initial emphasis on the status, or social role, of the plaintiff. Thus *Sullivan* was extended from public officials to "public figures."[16]

Such individuals, like public officials, have less claim on the First Amendment than others, reasoned the Court, because they have "voluntarily" chosen to enter the arena of public affairs, after having been forewarned of the risks to their reputations in doing so, and because they typically have their own means of responding to falsehoods and correcting misimpressions. The Court embraced this position in 1974, in the case of *Gertz v. Robert Welch, Inc.,* defining a public figure as: "For the most part those who attain this status have assumed roles of especial prominence in the affairs of society. Some occupy positions of such persuasive power and influence that they are deemed public figures for all purposes. More commonly, those classed as public figures have thrust themselves to the forefront of particular public controversies in order to influence the resolution of the issues involved."[17] "In either event," said the Court, "they invite attention and comment."[18]

In a series of ensuing cases, the Court began the process of defining what it means for a person to have "thrust themselves to the forefront of particular public controversies in order to influence the resolution of the issues involved." In every subsequent case in which the issue of public figure status has been contested, the Court has found insufficient evidence of the plaintiff having attained it. Hence, today we know more of what public figure status is not than of what it is. We know (from *Time v. Firestone*)[19] that a prominent Palm Beach socialite is not a public figure for that reason alone, nor for being sued for divorce on the grounds of adultery, nor for filing a counterclaim in that same action. She was deemed a private individual despite the fact that "the marital difficulties of extremely wealthy individuals may be of interest to some portion of the reading public"[20] and that she held press conferences during the trial. We know (from *Wolston v. Reader's Digest Ass'n*)[21] that a man cannot be considered a public figure just because sixteen years earlier he had refused to appear before a grand jury investigating Soviet espionage and had been convicted of contempt of court, events that were reported in Washington and New York newspapers at the time. And we know (from *Hutchinson v. Proxmire*)[22] that a director of a mental hospital is not a public figure because he obtained federal funding for research directed at establishing an "objective measure of aggression" through the study of the "clenching of jaws" of "certain animals."[23]

Over the past twenty-five years, the Court has also added many layers of rules to the basic holdings of *Sullivan* and *Gertz* that public officials and public figures must establish actual malice to recover for defamatory statements about them. The Court has held that these rules apply not just to statements made by the press but to the comments of others as well;[24] that states cannot permit private individuals to recover for defamatory statements if the press is "without fault";[25] that, "at least when a newspaper publishes speech of public concern," a private-figure plaintiff must bear the burden of proving falsity;[26] that, unless there is a finding of actual malice, states can impose liability only upon proof of "actual injury" (except in libel actions involving statements not about "issues of public concern");[27] and that states can award punitive damages only when actual malice occurred.[28] In its most recent ruling in the area of libel and the Constitution, the Court refused to create a special protection for statements of "opinion," but instead permitted states to examine all allegedly libelous statements to determine whether to the average reader they imply an assertion of fact that is defamatory.[29]

Throughout, the Court has continued to insist that the problem is one of finding the appropriate balance between the First Amendment's interest in uninhibited debate about public issues and the state's interest in protecting individual reputations. Its rulings have had ramifications in several different realms.

National Security

In 1971 the *Pentagon Papers* case[30] came before the Supreme Court. The Nixon administration had petitioned the federal courts to enjoin both the New York Times and the Washington Post from publishing portions of a classified report prepared in the Department of Defense entitled "History of U.S. Decision-making Process on Viet Nam Policy." The government claimed that publication would result in "the death of soldiers, the destruction of alliances, the greatly increased difficulty of negotiation with our enemies, [and] the inability of our diplomats to negotiate."[31] A majority of the Court held that claim to be insufficient, citing its rule that "[a]ny system of prior restraints of expression comes to this Court bearing a heavy presumption against its constitutional validity."[32] The government, it ruled, "had not met that burden."[33]

Public Access to the Press

In 1974, the Court in *Miami Herald Publishing Co. v. Tornillo*[34] considered a Florida statute that required newspapers within the state to publish without cost the reply of any candidate criticized in its columns. In a relatively brief and conclusory opinion, the Court surveyed prior print media cases and found implicit in them the proposition that "any . . . compulsion [by the government on newspapers] to publish that which 'reason' tells them should not be published is uncontstitutional."[35] Access regulation violates that principle because it intrudes "into the function of editors"[36] and because the justices assumed that, although there was no evidence on the point, it also creates an impermissible risk of a chilling effect on news content. The Court was emphatic in its ruling:

> Even if a newspaper would face no additional costs to comply with a compulsory access law and would not be forced to forego publication of news or opinion by the inclusion of a reply, the Florida statute fails to clear the barriers of the First Amendment because of its intrusion into the function of editors. A newspaper is more than a passive receptacle or conduit for news, comment, and advertising. The choice of material to go into a newspaper, and the decisions made as to limitations on the size and content of the paper, and treatment of public issues and public officials—whether fair or unfair—constitute the exercise of editiorial control and judgment. It has yet to be demonstrated how governmental regulation of this crucial process can be exercised consistent with First Amendment guarantees of a free press as they have evolved to this time.[37]

Invasion of Privacy

In 1975, in *Cox Broadcasting Corp. v. Cohn*,[38] the Court considered the constitutionality of a Georgia law that made publishing the name of a rape victim a misdemeanor. The defendant had reported the name of a woman who had been raped, having learned her identity when its reporter attended a hearing for those charged with the crime. Because the woman had been killed, her father sued, claiming that the publication of his daughter's identity as a rape victim had violated his privacy. He cited the statute as a legislative declaration that such information was not a matter of public concern. The Court held that this action against the press was prohibited by the First Amendment.

In its ruling the Court did recognize that "powerful arguments can be made and have been made, that however it may be ultimately defined, there *is* a zone of privacy surrounding every individual, a zone within which the State may protect him from intrusion by the press, with all its attendant publicity."[39] But, while the state's interest in preserving this zone of privacy was held to be substantial, so was the First Amendment interest in unencumbered discussion of public issues. Fortunately, the Court said, this "face-off" could be saved for another day. This case was decided on a much narrower issue, namely, "whether the State may impose sanctions on the accurate publication of the name of a rape victim obtained from public records—more specifically, from judicial records which are maintained in connection with a public prosecution and which themselves are open to public inspection."[40] To this question the answer was no.

In support of its conclusion, the Court argued as follows. The public depends on the press to be its eyes and ears when it comes to the affairs of government. "Great responsibility is accordingly placed upon the news media to report fully and accurately the proceedings of government, and official records and documents open to the public are the basic data of governmental operations."[41] In other words, this is considered to be significant information from a First Amendment standpoint. Since the people are sovereign, and since Georgia, by placing it in the public record, had deemed this information relevant to the administration of justice, and since the media serves as the eyes and ears of the public for these purposes, the press must be free to communicate such information to the citizenry. "At the very least," the Court stated, "The First and Fourteenth Amendments will not allow exposing the press to liability for truthfully publishing information released to the public in official court records."[42] On the other hand, although the Court would not guarantee its constitutionality, states were free to try to "avoid public documentation or other exposure of private information."[43]

In 1989 the Court in *Florida Star v. B.J.F.*[44] returned to the problem of state statutes forbidding the disclosure of the names of rape victims, overturning a finding of civil liability of a Jacksonville newspaper for publishing such a name. A reporter had learned the identity of the victim by reading a sheriff's report that was made freely available in the official press room.

In its ruling the Court began by noting that it had recently confronted "several" cases involving the "tension between the right which the First Amendment accords to a free press, on the one hand, and the protections which various statutes and common-law doctrines accord to personal privacy against the publication of truthful information, on the other."[45] The rule to be applied was this: "[I]f a newspaper lawfully obtains truthful information about a matter of public significance then state officials may not constitutionally punish publication of the information, absent a need to further a state interest of the highest order."[46]

The Court felt that this accorded adequate protection to both the press and the state. For the state, in particular, it was noted not only that a prohibition against publication of public facts was likely to be a fruitless gesture but also that the state had other adequate means of preserving the secrecy of harmful information:

> To the extent sensitive information rests in private hands, the government may under some circumstances forbid its nonconsensual acquisition. . . . To the extent sensitive information is in the government's custody, it has even greater power to forestall or mitigate the injury caused by its release. The government may classify certain information, establish and enforce procedures ensuring its

redacted release, and extend a damages remedy against the government or its officials where the government's mishandling of sensitive information leads to its dissemination. Where information is entrusted to the government, a less drastic means than punishing truthful publication almost always exists for guarding against the dissemination of private facts.[47]

The Court also expressed concern about the self-censorship the press would practice if it had to sift through publicly released state information to determine what was legally publishable.

In this case, since the newspaper had legally obtained information about the identity of the rape victim, and since its article clearly addressed "a matter of public significance," the state was required to come forward with a sufficient contrary interest. Florida claimed "the privacy of the victims of sexual offenses; the physical safety of such victims, who may be targeted for retaliation if their names become known to their assailants; and the goal of encouraging victims of such crimes to report these offenses without fear of exposure."[48] These are important interests, said the Court, but they are insufficient (for reasons given previously) in terms of the state's ability to use alternative methods to maintain secrecy and in terms of the undesirability of press self-censorship. The Court cited two additional reasons: that the Florida statute was overinclusive in punishing the press in instances where no harm would result from publication, and that it was underinclusive in punishing the press, but not others, who might distribute the information.

Intentional Infliction of Emotional Distress

In *Hustler Magazine, Inc. v. Falwell*,[49] the Court considered a claim of the well-known, fundamentalist minister Jerry Falwell that Hustler Magazine had intentionally published an "outrageous" parody of him and had thereby caused him to suffer deep "emotional distress." The parody consisted of a supposed advertisement (labeled "ad parody—not to be taken seriously") in which Falwell described his first sexual encounter as (in the Court's words) "a drunken incestuous rendezvous with his mother in an outhouse."[50] A jury had found this tortious and awarded Falwell $100,000 in compensatory damages and the same amount in punitive damages.

The Court reversed, finding the parody protected by the First Amendment. Falwell was a public figure, said the Court, and these statements were not reasonably understood as false assertions of fact and therefore could not be defamatory. Given that caricature has played a long and distinguished role in public debate in this country, and that it would be unduly threatening to that highly valuable form of expression to make an exception even for this kind of "distant cousin," the Court concluded that the speech was protected. Falwell's only claim was that it was proper for states to protect individuals, including public officials and public figures, against the pain inflicted by such intentional and "outrageous" commentary.

Taxation

In *Minneapolis Star and Tribune Co. v. Minnesota Commissioner of Revenue*,[51] the Court struck down a Minnesota tax on the ink and paper used in publishing newspapers. A special exemption within the tax resulted in only the larger state newspapers carrying the burden of payment. In fact, the Minneapolis Star and Tribune paid two-thirds of all the taxes collected each year. While the state had not intended the tax as a means of censoring newspapers, the Court saw a potential burden on the press and demanded that the state come forward with a compelling interest to justify a tax that fell differentially on members of the press. Imposing such a high burden on the state was necessary, the Court said, because a tax on only the press "can operate as effectively as a censor to check critical comment by the press, undercutting the basic assumption of our political system that the press will often serve as an important restraint on government."[52] The Court found the state's asserted justification for the special tax (to raise revenue through what essentially was a convenient variant of a general sales tax) was not compelling.

This case was followed four years later by *Arkansas Writers' Project, Inc. v. Ragland*,[53] in which the Court also held unconstitutional an Arkansas general sales tax that exempted some but not all newspapers and magazines. Among those not exempted was the plaintiff, which published a general interest monthly magazine called the Arkansas Times. In its ruling, the Court again expressed fear over the potential danger for state abuse of taxation that differentially favored or disfavored the press or certain members of it.

Free Press/Fair Trial

In 1976, in *Nebraska Press Association v. Stuart*,[54] the Court held unconstitutional a state court judge's order that restrained the press from publishing "strongly implicative" statements of guilt made by a defendant who had been indicted for the murder of six persons. The Court acknowledged that pretrial publicity might taint the judicial process but saw the First Amendment as commanding a strong presumption against such restraints on the press. Its holding was summarized as follows:

> The record demonstrates, as the Nebraska courts held, that there was indeed a risk that pretrial news accounts, true or false, would have some adverse impact on the attitudes of those who might be called as jurors. But on the record now before us it is not clear that further publicity, unchecked, would so distort the views of potential jurors that 12 could not be found who would, under proper instructions, fulfill their sworn duty to render a just verdict exclusively on the evidence presented in open court. We cannot say on this record that alternatives to a prior restraint on petitioners would not have sufficiently mitigated the adverse effects of pretrial publicity so as to make prior restraint unnecessary. Nor can we conclude that the restraining order actually entered would serve its intended purpose. Reasonable minds can have few doubts about the gravity of the evil pretrial publicity can work, but the probability that it would do so here was not demonstrated with the degree of certainty our cases on prior restraint require.[55]

In the end, the Court left little hope that states could ever show that these alternatives to a prior restraint were inadequate.

The Right to Gather News

After a fitful start, the Court has begun to develop a right of the press, and the public, to have access to newsworthy information and events, at least in the context of criminal proceedings. In 1980, in *Richmond Newspapers, Inc. v. Virginia*,[56] the Court held that the First Amendment guaranteed the press and the public the right to attend a murder trial that the trial judge had closed to the public at the defendant's request. Although there was no majority opinion, the plurality opinions stressed the fact that historically trials had been open proceedings, intended to insure public acceptance of and satisfaction with the results (the "community therapeutic value" of openness) and provide a deterrent to improper decision making.[57] Justice Brennan, in particular, emphasized the "structural" role of the First Amendment "in securing and fostering our republican system of self-government."[58]

Two years later, in *Globe Newspaper Co. v. Superior Court*,[59] the Court struck down a Massachusetts statute requiring courtrooms to be closed whenever a minor victim of a sexual crime was testifying. The Court insisted that the rule was too restrictive of First Amendment interests and that the state's interests in protecting the child and encouraging victims to come forward could be satisfied through a case-by-case approach. Further, the Court reasoned, since the state only prohibited the presence of the press in court, not the reading and reporting of transcripts, it was doubtful that the statute met the state's asserted interests.

The Court has since extended its rulings to support a newspaper's request to see the voir dire transcript in a murder trial (*Press-Enterprise Co. v. Superior Court*[60] [1984]); and to support the same newspaper's subsequent request to gain access to the transcripts of a preliminary hearing in a criminal prosecution (*Press-Enterprise Co. v. Superior Court*[61] [1986]). As it had previously, the Court in these cases recognized the possibility that the state might show compelling reasons justifying closure but insisted that specific findings were required. In the second *Press-Enterprise* case, it also ruled that such findings must demonstrate "first, there is a substantial probability that the defendant's right to a fair trial will be prejudiced by publicity that closure would prevent and, second, reasonable alternatives to closure cannot adequately protect the defendant's fair trial rights."[62]

The press has not always returned victorious from the field of battle between the First Amendment and the state. One notorious example was the highly controversial (within both the press and the Court) decision in *Branzburg v. Hayes.*[63] *Branzburg* was a case of the 1960s, though it was decided by the Court in 1972. In several different proceedings, reporters who had acquired knowledge of or witnessed criminal activities were called by prosecutors to appear before grand juries and testify as to what they had seen or knew. The reporters stated that they had promised not to divulge the identity of their sources. The First Amendment, they claimed, should protect them from having to violate those promises unless the state could show "that the reporter possesses information relevant to a crime the grand jury is investigating, that the information the reporter has is unavailable from other sources, and that the need for the information is sufficiently compelling to override the claimed invasion of First Amendment interests occasioned by the disclosure."[64] Such a qualified "privilege" was needed, the reporters argued, because confidential sources are essential to the gathering of news, which in turn is essential to the reporting of news to the public. No one, they argued, could doubt the public value of information about criminal activity.

Branzburg was actually a combination of three cases. In the first, a reporter had written articles for his newspaper about drug use and the making of hashish, claiming to have personally observed these activities. In the second case, a reporter had been present in the local headquarters of the Black Panther Party when a police raid was expected. And in the third case, a reporter had interviewed members of the Black Panther Party about the group's activities.

The Supreme Court rejected the reporters' claim of a First Amendment privilege not to testify before a grand jury. With policy. Within this perspective are those who would abolish the system of public regulation of electronic media entirely. Finally, there are others, standing somewhere in the middle, who propose that the overall situation stay more or less as it is. Theirs tends to be a search for justifications for this system of differential treatment of the print and electronic media, a quest to identify material differences between the two.

I have a rather full agenda with regard to these debates. I wish to show, first of all, that freedom of the press is not nearly so simple as the *Sullivan* model—its theory and its cases—would have us presume. As for the potential for press abuse of its freedoms, there are important moderating influences to be considered. One is the role of the courts, especially the Supreme Court, in shaping how the society, and the press, conceives of the proper use of that freedom. The other is the system of public regulation of the electronic media. This remarkable experiment has involved not only extensive public regulation of the press but also reflected a radically new vision of the role of law and the press. We must consider the extent to which that system has influenced the development of the *Sullivan* model. We must also consider the converse possibility: that the *Sullivan* model has operated to influence developments within the system of public regulation for new communications technologies.

There are, therefore, substantial questions as to whether opting exclusively for either an autonomy model or a public regulation model will alter the balance heretofore maintained between these reciprocally influencing experiments.

Next, focusing more particularly on the experiment of public regulation in the context of electronic media, I have three primary objectives. The first is to offer a theory for a system of partial regulation, a system such as we have had with the newer media regulated and the print media preserved largely unregulated. My argument is that this is a rational system, both as a matter of constitutional law and as a matter of public policy, even though there may be no significant differences between the regulated and unregulated media. The second is to show how thus far there has been an inadequate assessment of the experience with public regulation of the electronic media. And the third aim is to distinguish between several theories for public

the announced attitude that it could not "seriously entertain" the notion that "it is better to write about crime than to do something about it,"[65] the Court relied on arguments that the common law had refused in the past to find such a privilege, that it woulde be unwise to grant the press a First Amendment right the rest of the public does not enjoy (in part because of the ensuing difficulties of defining "the press"), and that the evidence was not compelling that reporters' sources would disappear without such a privilege.

The press was partially unsuccessful in another of its claims for a special constitutional privilege, this time for protection against government searches of newsrooms. In *Zurcher v. Stanford Daily*,[66] the police had obtained a warrant to search the campus newspaper's offices in order to seize photographs that might help identify individuals who had assaulted police officers during a violent demonstration. Writing for the Court, Justice White dismissed the press's fear that the government would take advantage of its power to search newsrooms and examine or seize other confidential press documents, thereby discouraging effective newsgathering.[67] That, said Justice White, was an unrealistic fear, since experience showed that police seldom conduct newsroom searches: "This reality hardly suggests abuse, and if abuse occurs, there will be time enough to deal with it."[68]

As in *Branzburg*, Justice Powell's was the fifth and therefore deciding vote in *Zurcher*. His concurring opinions in both cases left the constitutional waters of press privileges somewhat murky when he said that, in deciding whether to compel a reporter to testify before a grand jury or whether to permit a newsroom search, courts should take account of "the independent values protected by the First Amendment."[69]

III

That the press may thus far have been largely unsuccessful in persuading the Court to create special First Amendment privileges for journalists does not, however, mean that the press has been unsuccessful in inducing the Court to recognize the press's special role in the American political system and to shape First

Amendment doctrine accordingly. Even when First Amendment rights are created equally for both the press and the general public, the stimulus may be a special concern for the press. The cases reviewed in this chapter suggest that this indeed has been true. The press and the public may have the same right to attend criminal trials, but it is the press that will actually take advantage of the right and in doing so fulfill its purposes (as conceived by the Court). And though the Court's analysis in *New York Times v. Sullivan* never emphasized the fact that the case involved the press, any alert reader of the Court's opinion will sense how significant that fact was to how the law was ultimately fashioned. Further, we have seen how frequently one encounters judicial observations about the press's special role in fulfilling the *Sullivan* conception. Only the press, it is commonly noted, has the capacity to do business on an equal footing with the government, to inform the public, and to facilitate the exchange of public opinion. The First Amendment history of the last three decades is one that includes an ever-growing consciousness of the positive benefits of press freedom.[70]

Since *New York Times v. Sullivan*, therefore, there has arisen a jurisprudence of and for the press. That jurisprudence flows from the central image, or intellectual framework, of *Sullivan* and the special niche in that image for the press. The critical features of the image are these: the government is untrustworthy when it comes to regulating public debate, for it will forever try to recapture its authoritarian powers through laws such as seditious libel. The citizens, on the other hand, must be regarded and trusted as the ultimate sovereign. Open debate must be preserved for their benefit. In this scheme, the press is the public's representative, its agent, helping stand guard against the atavistic tendencies of the state and serving as a forum for public discussion.[71]

To implement this intellectual framework, the Court, as we have now seen, has developed several doctrinal strategies: from the strong presumption that the government will abuse any authority it possesses over the press, there arises the insistence that the government be kept at some considerable distance from the press. Even when the government's interests for regulation are strong, the Court will make its own assessment to determine

how compelling they are; insist that the government first t means other than regulation of the press to satisfy those intere and require the state to proceed on a case-by-case basis rat than by general rule.

This, then, is what we generally believe to be the foundat of the modern principle of freedom of the press. Though it n be still in its infancy, it has already established a solid base press liberty. From the Warren Court to the Burger Court to Rehnquist Court, the press has achieved a record of suc matched by few other litigants before the Court. It is true too and has been true for some time, that whenever public reg tion touches the press the alarm will be sounded. And the r conventional cry will issue that, when it comes to the press, government must keep its hands off.

IV

Before proceeding, it might be helpful for some readers to a general map of the terrain covered in the succeeding chap I do so with some reluctance, however, because a major tl of this book is that the reality of press freedom in this coun significantly more complex than the *Sullivan* conception cates *and*, further, that this complexity is surprisingly una ciated. By offering now a survey of what follows, there is loss to the narrative—and substantive—power of seeing complexity unfold gradually. For those readers, therefore, feel little need for outlines, I suggest moving on to the chapter now.

Today strong currents of thought criss-cross the sea of dom of the press. Some articulate the fear that *Sullivan* a legacy leave too much power with the press, too much o tunity for abuse. Within this perspective are those who favorably on the extraordinary and extensive system of regulation that has covered the electronic media for over a century, and who propose that a part or all of that syste extended to the unregulated print media. Others find this gether wrong-headed. They see that system of regulati constitutionally unjustified or as unwise as a matter of regulation of the media and to propose one in particular as the most reasonable and consistent with evolving First Amendment traditions.

This leads me, finally, to a general discussion of the changes I see occurring with the overall conception of the idea of a free press. There is a need for clearer working images. We should think of the model of *New York Times v. Sullivan* as only one end of an acceptable spectrum of possibilities for approaching the concept of freedom of the press. At the other end, I suggest the need to begin to develop a more sophisticated model of quality public debate, in which there is some room for public institutions to be used to help moderate tendencies within everyone that distort and bias the process of public discussion and decision making. At present, we are at neither end but positioned somewhere in the middle. In my view, not only should we recognize that fact, but we should also be prepared to engage in open debate about how much farther along that spectrum—toward the image of quality debate—the society can afford to move.

CHAPTER TWO

The Costs of an Autonomous Press

W hat should concern us about this principle of press autonomy initiated by *New York Times v. Sullivan* and
fulfilled by its progeny? I take up that question here and consider, too, how well the Court has evaluated those concerns as it
has set about building our system of press freedom. At the moment, I am not interested in considering the variety of potential
remedial actions for dealing with these problems, their effectiveness, and their costs, or in comparing those to the net benefits
that might be claimed for the autonomy approach. While it is
possible that, on balance, autonomy is the best system available,
superior to any form of public regulation we might imagine, we
are still at the preliminary stage of beginning to think about the
risks and costs of the present system. Later, those costs can be set
against the benefits claimed for it by *Sullivan* and its sequels, and
then a comparison to other approaches will be possible.

I

The idea of journalistic autonomy can be criticized on many
different grounds. The most obvious is that this degree of press
freedom requires too great a sacrifice of competing *social* interests. This leads us to ask what those interests are and whether the
Court has properly assessed them. If it has not, we then will
want to know what explains this undervaluation or misjudgment.

Let us begin with the most conventional form of criticism of
press autonomy. It is possible to claim—and some have done
so—that the Court has purchased press freedom at too high a

the announced attitude that it could not "seriously entertain" the notion that "it is better to write about crime than to do something about it,"[65] the Court relied on arguments that the common law had refused in the past to find such a privilege, that it woulde be unwise to grant the press a First Amendment right the rest of the public does not enjoy (in part because of the ensuing difficulties of defining "the press"), and that the evidence was not compelling that reporters' sources would disappear without such a privilege.

The press was partially unsuccessful in another of its claims for a special constitutional privilege, this time for protection against government searches of newsrooms. In *Zurcher v. Stanford Daily*,[66] the police had obtained a warrant to search the campus newspaper's offices in order to seize photographs that might help identify individuals who had assaulted police officers during a violent demonstration. Writing for the Court, Justice White dismissed the press's fear that the government would take advantage of its power to search newsrooms and examine or seize other confidential press documents, thereby discouraging effective newsgathering.[67] That, said Justice White, was an unrealistic fear, since experience showed that police seldom conduct newsroom searches: "This reality hardly suggests abuse, and if abuse occurs, there will be time enough to deal with it."[68]

As in *Branzburg*, Justice Powell's was the fifth and therefore deciding vote in *Zurcher*. His concurring opinions in both cases left the constitutional waters of press privileges somewhat murky when he said that, in deciding whether to compel a reporter to testify before a grand jury or whether to permit a newsroom search, courts should take account of "the independent values protected by the First Amendment."[69]

III

That the press may thus far have been largely unsuccessful in persuading the Court to create special First Amendment privileges for journalists does not, however, mean that the press has been unsuccessful in inducing the Court to recognize the press's special role in the American political system and to shape First

Amendment doctrine accordingly. Even when First Amendment rights are created equally for both the press and the general public, the stimulus may be a special concern for the press. The cases reviewed in this chapter suggest that this indeed has been true. The press and the public may have the same right to attend criminal trials, but it is the press that will actually take advantage of the right and in doing so fulfill its purposes (as conceived by the Court). And though the Court's analysis in *New York Times v. Sullivan* never emphasized the fact that the case involved the press, any alert reader of the Court's opinion will sense how significant that fact was to how the law was ultimately fashioned. Further, we have seen how frequently one encounters judicial observations about the press's special role in fulfilling the *Sullivan* conception. Only the press, it is commonly noted, has the capacity to do business on an equal footing with the government, to inform the public, and to facilitate the exchange of public opinion. The First Amendment history of the last three decades is one that includes an ever-growing consciousness of the positive benefits of press freedom.[70]

Since *New York Times v. Sullivan*, therefore, there has arisen a jurisprudence of and for the press. That jurisprudence flows from the central image, or intellectual framework, of *Sullivan* and the special niche in that image for the press. The critical features of the image are these: the government is untrustworthy when it comes to regulating public debate, for it will forever try to recapture its authoritarian powers through laws such as seditious libel. The citizens, on the other hand, must be regarded and trusted as the ultimate sovereign. Open debate must be preserved for their benefit. In this scheme, the press is the public's representative, its agent, helping stand guard against the atavistic tendencies of the state and serving as a forum for public discussion.[71]

To implement this intellectual framework, the Court, as we have now seen, has developed several doctrinal strategies: from the strong presumption that the government will abuse any authority it possesses over the press, there arises the insistence that the government be kept at some considerable distance from the press. Even when the government's interests for regulation are strong, the Court will make its own assessment to determine how compelling they are; insist that the government first try means other than regulation of the press to satisfy those interests; and require the state to proceed on a case-by-case basis rather than by general rule.

This, then, is what we generally believe to be the foundation of the modern principle of freedom of the press. Though it may be still in its infancy, it has already established a solid base for press liberty. From the Warren Court to the Burger Court to the Rehnquist Court, the press has achieved a record of success matched by few other litigants before the Court. It is true today, and has been true for some time, that whenever public regulation touches the press the alarm will be sounded. And the now conventional cry will issue that, when it comes to the press, the government must keep its hands off.

IV

Before proceeding, it might be helpful for some readers to have a general map of the terrain covered in the succeeding chapters. I do so with some reluctance, however, because a major theme of this book is that the reality of press freedom in this country is significantly more complex than the *Sullivan* conception indicates *and*, further, that this complexity is surprisingly unappreciated. By offering now a survey of what follows, there is some loss to the narrative—and substantive—power of seeing that complexity unfold gradually. For those readers, therefore, who feel little need for outlines, I suggest moving on to the next chapter now.

Today strong currents of thought criss-cross the sea of freedom of the press. Some articulate the fear that *Sullivan* and its legacy leave too much power with the press, too much opportunity for abuse. Within this perspective are those who look favorably on the extraordinary and extensive system of public regulation that has covered the electronic media for over a half-century, and who propose that a part or all of that system be extended to the unregulated print media. Others find this altogether wrong-headed. They see that system of regulation as constitutionally unjustified or as unwise as a matter of public policy. Within this perspective are those who would abolish the system of public regulation of electronic media entirely. Finally, there are others, standing somewhere in the middle, who propose that the overall situation stay more or less as it is. Theirs tends to be a search for justifications for this system of differential treatment of the print and electronic media, a quest to identify material differences between the two.

I have a rather full agenda with regard to these debates. I wish to show, first of all, that freedom of the press is not nearly so simple as the *Sullivan* model—its theory and its cases—would have us presume. As for the potential for press abuse of its freedoms, there are important moderating influences to be considered. One is the role of the courts, especially the Supreme Court, in shaping how the society, and the press, conceives of the proper use of that freedom. The other is the system of public regulation of the electronic media. This remarkable experiment has involved not only extensive public regulation of the press but also reflected a radically new vision of the role of law and the press. We must consider the extent to which that system has influenced the development of the *Sullivan* model. We must also consider the converse possibility: that the *Sullivan* model has operated to influence developments within the system of public regulation for new communications technologies.

There are, therefore, substantial questions as to whether opting exclusively for either an autonomy model or a public regulation model will alter the balance heretofore maintained between these reciprocally influencing experiments.

Next, focusing more particularly on the experiment of public regulation in the context of electronic media, I have three primary objectives. The first is to offer a theory for a system of partial regulation, a system such as we have had with the newer media regulated and the print media preserved largely unregulated. My argument is that this is a rational system, both as a matter of constitutional law and as a matter of public policy, even though there may be no significant differences between the regulated and unregulated media. The second is to show how thus far there has been an inadequate assessment of the experience with public regulation of the electronic media. And the third aim is to distinguish between several theories for public regulation of the media and to propose one in particular as the most reasonable and consistent with evolving First Amendment traditions.

This leads me, finally, to a general discussion of the changes I see occurring with the overall conception of the idea of a free press. There is a need for clearer working images. We should think of the model of *New York Times v. Sullivan* as only one end of an acceptable spectrum of possibilities for approaching the concept of freedom of the press. At the other end, I suggest the need to begin to develop a more sophisticated model of quality public debate, in which there is some room for public institutions to be used to help moderate tendencies within everyone that distort and bias the process of public discussion and decision making. At present, we are at neither end but positioned somewhere in the middle. In my view, not only should we recognize that fact, but we should also be prepared to engage in open debate about how much farther along that spectrum—toward the image of quality debate—the society can afford to move.

The Costs of an Autonomous Press

W hat should concern us about this principle of press autonomy initiated by *New York Times v. Sullivan* and fulfilled by its progeny? I take up that question here and consider, too, how well the Court has evaluated those concerns as it has set about building our system of press freedom. At the moment, I am not interested in considering the variety of potential remedial actions for dealing with these problems, their effectiveness, and their costs, or in comparing those to the net benefits that might be claimed for the autonomy approach. While it is possible that, on balance, autonomy is the best system available, superior to any form of public regulation we might imagine, we are still at the preliminary stage of beginning to think about the risks and costs of the present system. Later, those costs can be set against the benefits claimed for it by *Sullivan* and its sequels, and then a comparison to other approaches will be possible.

I

The idea of journalistic autonomy can be criticized on many different grounds. The most obvious is that this degree of press freedom requires too great a sacrifice of competing *social* interests. This leads us to ask what those interests are and whether the Court has properly assessed them. If it has not, we then will want to know what explains this undervaluation or misjudgment.

Let us begin with the most conventional form of criticism of press autonomy. It is possible to claim—and some have done so—that the Court has purchased press freedom at too high a price of human pain suffered by individuals who, for example, have their reputations sullied by defamatory statements or by disclosures of private personal facts. If the price has indeed been too high, one possible explanation might be that (taking the libel area) the Court got off to a bad start when it established a general rule based on the particular facts of *Sullivan*. *Sullivan* was surely not a representative libel case. It seems doubtful that Mr. Sullivan's reputation was seriously damaged by the allegedly false statements in the New York Times advertisement. Indeed, given the time and the place, it is not inconceivable that his reputation was enhanced by it. It is a commonly observed fact among lawyers that the outcome of a case may depend upon the special features of the litigants before a court (creating the "central image," as it were, of what the world is like for purposes of a particular ruling). It is highly desirable, psychologically, to have a sympathetic client. And when the *Sullivan* case was called before the Supreme Court, Sullivan's lawyer must have known he didn't have one. Because not every public official is a Sullivan, it is reasonable to ask whether in adopting the rules it did covering public debate generally the Court's judgment about the human costs involved was distorted by the peculiar facts before it at the time.

There is a further sign in the libel case law that this has in fact occurred. It will be recalled from the discussion in Chapter 1 that the Court has continued to insist that public officials and figures cannot legitimately complain about the lack of legal protection against defamatory statements under *Sullivan* because they have "voluntarily" chosen to enter the arena of public debate and have, therefore, "assumed the risk" of nasty commentary. This, however, is an unfair ploy by the Court, an avoidance maneuver by which it tries to minimize the degree to which we should care about the pain inflicted under our rules. Essentially, the Court has said that, since these individuals have freely chosen a public life, what happens to them is their own doing, just as it is for a man who breaks his leg while hiking in the wilderness. Putting aside for the moment the fact that we also have an interest in encouraging people to enter public affairs, it simply is wrong to suppose that the pain inflicted by defamatory statements about public officials and figures is not our responsibility or concern.

It should always be open to people to object to the way the world works under the rules we create, and not be dismissed by the claim that they have chosen to continue living in that world and, therefore, can be taken as having assented to it.

There are several other examples of the Supreme Court undervaluing the private costs of press speech. Consider the Court's analysis of the privacy interests at stake in *Cox Broadcasting* and *Florida Star*, discussed in Chapter 1. The Court there intimated that states had no serious cognizable interest in preserving the anonymity of rape victims in the context of the mass media once the information about identity was made available to any member or segment of the public. The Court thus seemed to indicate that any disclosure eliminates all privacy interests at stake. But a Court sensitive to the privacy costs involved surely would have noted that to a normal person there is a great difference between having a humiliating and embarrassing fact recorded in a transcript housed at the local courthouse and having it become the headline of the local newspaper or television station.

These and similar instances suggest that we should worry about whether the Court has been sufficiently attentive to the competing human costs wrought by the principle of an autonomous, unregulated press as it has evolved in recent decades.

But as important as this concern is about the minimization of the private interests sacrificed to the principle of press autonomy, there are even more serious matters to worry about. We must also consider how press freedom might, instead of enhancing public discussion and decision making, actually prove to be a threat to it—a threat to quality decision making, a threat to *democracy*, a threat to the very values the First Amendment (as defined by *New York Times v. Sullivan* and its successors) is supposed to further.

There is no guarantee that the press will not abuse the freedom it possesses under the autonomy model. And there are many ways in which it might do so. The press can exclude important points of view, operating as a bottleneck in the marketplace of ideas. It can distort knowledge of public issues not just by omission but also through active misrepresentations and lies. It can also exert an adverse influence over the tone and character of public debate in subtle ways, by playing to personal biases and prejudices or by making people fearful and, therefore, desirous of strong authority. It can fuel ignorance and pettiness by avoiding public issues altogether, favoring simple-minded fare or cheap entertainment over serious discussion. Even if the pressures for low-quality discussion come from the people themselves, as to some extent they do, the press acts harmfully by responding to those demands and hence satisfying and reinforcing them. It matters not whether the press is the instigator of what is bad or the satisfier of inappropriate demands originating in the people. In either case, the press can be an appropriate locus for reform.

Of course, all these concerns become more serious as the number of those who control the press become fewer, and as more and more members of the general population turn to a few outlets for information about the world—both phenomena having undeniably occurred in the twentieth century. The value the First Amendment places on many speakers is not based on a premise that more speakers result in less bias in any one, rather it is assumed that more speakers mean more people who have a self-interest in correcting the biases of others, despite the fact that they are biased themselves. As the number of those who control the gateway to public discussion decreases, this natural corrective is lost. It is, of course, a widely known fact of this century that, for example, the total number of daily newspapers has declined sharply[1] and that the number of towns and cities across the country with competing papers has been reduced to a mere handful.[2] Coupled with this phenomenon is the increased reliance by citizens on massive media enterprises for information about the world.

These would seem to be the sorts of worries that ought to command our attention.

II

Shortly after the Second World War there appeared a major report on the condition of press freedom in the United States. *A*

27

Free and Responsible Press is a notable document, remarkable for the distinction of its authors, for its willingness to be critical of the press—and for its neglect by the contemporary world.

Published in 1947, the report was the work of the Commission on Freedom of the Press, a commission chaired by Robert M. Hutchins, the famous chancellor of the University of Chicago.[3] The commission was formed in 1943, with grants from Time, Inc., and Encyclopaedia Britannica, Inc., administered by the University of Chicago. Serving on the commission (in addition to Hutchins) were twelve eminent educators and public officials including Harold Lasswell (professor of law at Yale), Reinhold Niebuhr (professor of ethics and philosophy at Union Theological Seminary), and Beardsley Ruml (chairman of the Federal Reserve Bank of New York). The leading First Amendment scholar of this century, Zechariah Chafee, Jr., served as vice-chairman. The commission "heard testimony from 58 men and women connected with the press. The staff has recorded interviews with more than 225 members of the industries, government, and private agencies concerned with the press. The Commission held 17 two-day or three-day meetings and studied 176 documents prepared by its members or the staff."[4] Its aim was to study "the role of the agencies of mass communication in the education of the people in public affairs."[5]

Elegant, intelligent, and concise, the commission's report is as good a statement as we have of why the press is so important for the quality of our political system and why its freedom may be in jeopardy due to its inadequacies and abuses.

The report opens with a central question: "Is the freedom of the press in danger?" "Yes," it answers, and for three reasons:

> First, the importance of the press to the people has greatly increased with the development of the press as an instrument of mass communication. At the same time the development of the press as an instrument of mass communication has greatly decreased the proportion of the people who can express their opinions and ideas through the press.
>
> Second, the few who are able to use the machinery of the

press as an instrument of mass communication have not provided a service adequate to the needs of the society.

Third, those who direct the machinery of the press have engaged from time to time in practices which the society condemns and which, if continued, it will inevitably undertake to regulate or control.[6]

In the commission's view, it was a sad fact of modern life that, although an "extraordinarily high quality of performance has been achieved by the leaders in each field of mass communications," when we look "at the press as a whole" we must "conclude that it is not meeting the needs of our society."[7] Yet the public seemed unaware of this general failure.

What is needed, first of all, is recognition by the American people of the vital importance of the press in the present world crisis. We have the impression that the American people do not realize what has happened to them. They are not aware that the communications revolution has occurred. They do not appreciate the tremendous power which the new instruments and the new organization of the press place in the hands of a few men. They have not yet understood how far the performance of the press falls short of the requirements of a free society in the world today. The principal object of our report is to make these points clear.[8]

The commission said the problems with the modern press stemmed from the fact that the nature of the press has changed dramatically, that a "communications revolution has occurred."[9] The central characteristics of that revolution are the concentration of ownership and control in fewer and fewer hands and the growing dependence of the public on press agencies for information about the world. When the First Amendment was adopted, and for many decades thereafter, there were so many outlets that "anybody with anything to say had comparatively little difficulty in getting it published."[10] "Presses were cheap; the journeyman printer could become a publisher and editor by borrowing the few dollars he needed to set up his shop and by hiring an assistant or two. With a limited number of people who could read, and with property qualifications for the suffrage—less than 6 per cent of the adult population voted for the conventions held to ratify the Constitution—there was no great discrepancy between the number of those who could read and were active citizens and those who could command the financial resources to engage in publication."[11] Each publisher could indulge his or her prejudices, without harm to the public weal, because "in each village and town, with its relatively simple social structure and its wealth of neighborly contacts, various opinions might encounter each other in face-to-face meetings; the truth, it was hoped, would be sorted out by competition in the local market place."[12]

But today things are different. The press has become a massive enterprise, slouching toward monopoly. Even at the time of the commission report, more than forty years ago, "[n]inety-two per cent of the communities in this country, all but the bigger cities, have only one local newspaper."[13]

The power of the few to reach so many was the product of many converging forces: the invention of communications technology that increased the size of the reachable audience; the "advantages inherent in operating on a large scale using the new technology"[14] (what we refer to as economies of scale); the personal interest in power of press managers; and the practical necessity of very large enterprises to undertake the tasks of reporting on equally large enterprises, the largest, of course, being the government.

This state of affairs in modern communications could be used for either good or bad purposes. Intrinsically, it was not one or the other. But to evaluate press performance you have to know what you want. The commission thought we ought to want "first, a truthful, comprehensive, and intelligent account of the day's events in a context which gives them meaning; second, a forum for the exchange of comment and criticism; third, a means of projecting the opinions and attitudes of the groups in the society to one another; fourth, a method of presenting and clarifying the goals and values of the society; and, fifth, a way of reaching every member of the society by the currents of information, thought, and feeling which the press supplies."[15] Two features of the commission's report should be especially noted here. For the second requirement of a good press, noted above, it recommended that the "great agencies of mass communications should regard themselves as common carriers of public discussion."[16] In an ideal world, it said, there would be "general media, inevitably solicitous to present their own views, but setting forth other views fairly," and then "[a]s checks on their fairness, and partial safeguards against ignoring important matters, more specialized media of advocacy."[17] As to the third requirement, the commission specifically recognized the phenomenon of the central image and of the press's power to shape it. Mass media, it argued, must present a balanced and full portrait of groups within the society because "[p]eople make decisions in large part in terms of favorable or unfavorable images. They relate fact and opinion to stereotypes. . . . When the images [that the media] portray fail to present the social group truly, they tend to pervert judgment."[18]

What, then, for the commission, was the level of performance of the press as measured on this scale of values? How close had it come to meeting the needs of society? Technologically superior, reaching a wider audience, the American press was "less venal and less subservient to political and economic pressure than that of many other countries."[19] And the "leading organs of the American press have achieved a standard of excellence unsurpassed anywhere in the world."[20] But examined as a whole, society's needs were not being met:

> The news is twisted by the emphasis on firstness, on the novel and sensational; by the personal interests of owners; and by pressure groups. Too much of the regular output of the press consists of a miscellaneous succession of stories and images which have no relation to the typical lives of real people anywhere. Too often the result is meaninglessness, flatness, distortion, and the perpetuation of misunderstanding among widely scattered groups whose only contact is through these media.[21]

Many forces contending for control of content steer the press away from performing its important social role. The "economic logic of private enterprise forces most units of the mass communications industry to seek an ever larger audience," with the result being "an omnibus product which includes something for everybody."[22] "The American newspaper is now as much a medium of entertainment, specialized information, and advertising as it is of news."[23] "To attract the maximum audience, the press emphasizes the exceptional rather than the representative, the sensational rather than the significant."[24]

> Many activities of the utmost social consequence lie below the surface of what are conventionally regarded as reportable incidents: more power machinery; fewer men tending machines; more hours of leisure; more schooling per child; decrease of intolerance; successful negotiation of labor contracts; increase of participation in music through the schools; increase in the sale of books of biography and history.
>
> In most news media such matters are crowded out by stories of night-club murders, race riots, strike violence, and quarrels among public officials. The Commission does not object to the reporting of these incidents but to the preoccupation of the press with them. The press is preoccupied with them to such an extent that the citizen is not supplied the information and discussion he needs to discharge his responsibilities to the community.[25]

Additionally, the media were continuously exposed to the undesirable and self-serving pressures of groups within the audience, of their own biases as "big business," and of advertisers. And by "a kind of unwritten law the press ignores the errors and misrepresentations, the lies and scandals, of which its members are guilty."[26]

The commission stopped short of calling for government regulation. But such involvement clearly was not unthinkable. Freedom of the press, it said again and again, ought to be viewed as a "conditional right," one extended by society because of the advantages an autonomous press might provide. For press freedom to work, the society must possess a certain *"public mentality"*—"a mentality accustomed to the noise and confusion of clashing opinions and reasonably stable in temper in view of the varying fortunes of ideas."[27] But while these psychological conditions must exist in the society, they may be destroyed as well as created by the press itself. Press freedom has, the commission argued, both "moral" and "legal" dimensions, and they need not be coextensive.[28] Although the "moral" right might be "forfeited" through lying or other irresponsible speech, the "legal" right might still be "retained." Life with a cure may be worse than life with the disease. Circumstances, however, may change. The "legal right will stand unaltered as its moral duty is performed." But "[n]o democracy, . . . certainly not the American democracy, will indefinitely tolerate concentrations of private power irresponsible and strong enough to thwart the aspirations of the people."[29]

The commission recommended that self-regulation be tried first. At the time, the press was engaging in little internal regulation. To have a "profession" is to have a collective conscience, the commission observed. Yet, unlike the professions of law, medicine, and divinity, the press had not organized itself to define and cultivate its own standards. Journalism schools were failing in this, too.

The commission rejected the argument that the press could do no more than meet the demands of its audience, whatever they may be. "The agencies of mass communication," it argued, "are not serving static wants. Year by year they are building and transforming the interests of the public. They have an obligation to elevate rather than to degrade them."[30] The root of the dilemma, the commission warned, lay in "the way in which the press looks at itself." It must view itself as "performing a public service of a professional kind," and understand that "there are some things which a truly professional [person] will not do for money."[31]

To this general recommendation for self-reform, the commission added a few suggestions here and there, calling in the end for the creation of an independent body, funded privately, that would investigate and evaluate the performance of the press and issue reports of its findings and conclusions.

Such was the distinguished commission's analysis of the

state of affairs in the postwar press and of what was needed to create both a free and a responsible press.[32]

III

The report of the Commission on Freedom of the Press is not unique in modern times either in its warnings or in the remedies it proposed. There have been other, similar reports and critiques.[33] But the commission report is one of the most forcefully presented, and it reflects the considered judgment of a highly respected group of individuals. It also emerged at the beginning of the post–World War II era, which is of primary concern here, for that is when the phenomenon of mass communications took a giant leap forward, when people suddenly became intensely conscious of the potential totalitarian uses of mass communications,[34] and when the Supreme Court itself began dealing with a variety of government regulations that had a special or exclusive effect on the press. It was also a time when a major body of social science scholarship began to develop, one that continues to this day, seeking to understand how news media "construct" the news, how news production is affected, or skewed, by the economic structure of the society and the media, by the internal organizational structure of the media, and by broad cultural forces.[35] It is important to understand how the Supreme Court addressed and evaluated these concerns about the press as it set about developing the principle of autonomy described in Chapter 1.

To inquire into this matter is to confront the surprising fact that in virtually none of the cases referred to in Chapter 1 is there any serious treatment of the kind of concerns about the performance of the press one sees discussed in the commission report. The Court's failure to address these matters was not for want of opportunity. Indeed, in many cases it seems to have gone out of its way—to the brink of misrepresentation—to ignore the risk that the press can become a threat to democracy rather than its servant. All things considered, the Court's seemingly narrow-minded performance in this respect appears nothing short of astonishing.

Two areas of the law governing the press that display this

tendency of judicial avoidance are libel and privacy. In cases like *Sullivan* and *Cox Broadcasting,* it will be recalled, the Court has treated the costs of speech that is defamatory and invasive of privacy as purely *private,* the infliction of pain and suffering on individuals whose reputations in the community are tarnished by falsehoods or truths. The state's interest in prohibiting such speech is said to derive from the individual interest at stake.

While the individual interest in the areas of libel and invasion of privacy should not be belittled, to conceive of this as the only interest jeopardized by such speech is to ignore the relevance of other strong social concerns about the quality of public discussion. The Court in *Sullivan* began to develop an understanding of the psychology of speech behavior that is relevant to thinking about the First Amendment implications of laws such as those concerning defamation. Recall that the Court offered two competing images—the image of citizens reluctant to enter politics, and the image of them as uncontrollably aggressive when they do engage in political debate. Yet, despite the fact that the Court itself assumed these behavior patterns to be common, and despite the fact that both personality types might produce harmful effects for public discussion and decision making, a situation with ramifications well beyond the mere generation of libelous remarks, the Court gave no hint of recognition of that dimension of the problem, no hint of recognition that it might be dealing with an aspect of behavior that could thwart democracy unless curtailed. One would think that, given the premises about human nature the Court assumed, it would have been alerted to the fact that it was touching upon deeper and more complex issues.

In cases like *New York Times v. Sullivan,* therefore, the Court has essentially *privatized* the injury of speech behavior. But it does not take a great deal of imagination to discover why a concern with the quality of public discussion and decision making ought to extend to libelous utterances. We all have an interest in not being misled by falsehoods, including those about public officials or public figures. Otherwise, good public officials may be wrongly voted out of office or lose their capacity to persuade and lead those they represent, and the public may be led to make incorrect political judgments, all because the press reported a defamatory accusation. Journalism unrestrained by defamation law also may discourage citizens from entering political life, because they know they will have to bear the risk of libelous falsehoods without recourse against those who, though undeterred now from entering public debate, are similarly undeterred from making false accusations due to the lack of a potential action for damages. Those who choose to remain on the sidelines of public affairs may well be better people than those who become political actors.[36]

No mention of these concerns is to be found in the Court's opinion in *New York Times v. Sullivan,* or for that matter in any of its subsequent decisions. In *Sullivan* itself, the tremendous power of the institutional press is rhetorically avoided by not mentioning the press and by analyzing the case in terms of the far less menacing image of the "citizen critic." Even First Amendment analysts sensitive to the need for quality public discussion seem intent on avoiding the issue of the adverse effects on public discussion of uninhibited defamatory statements.

This neglect of the public interest has also occurred in the Court's limited foray into the law prohibiting publication of private facts, although here the story is somewhat more complicated and, in a sense, more interesting. I noted earlier that the Court's characterization of the cost of this kind of speech has been essentially that it is a matter of private pain and suffering. Yet, if one returns to the origins of the privacy concept, a very different analysis is found of the reasons for legal restrictions on privacy invasions.[37] In 1890, Samuel Warren and Louis Brandeis published the first plea for the creation of a right of action for invasions of privacy. Their essay was not an obscure law review article when it was published, nor is it now dusty with time and long forgotten. It was widely influential in its own time and even today is often described as the most famous law review article ever written. In it, Warren and Brandeis were concerned about providing legal redress to individuals whose privacy was invaded by the publication of personal facts. That is how the Court, in *Cox Broadcasting,* referred to it. But Warren and Brandeis also argued that the real destructiveness of the publication of private facts lay in its impact on *social* thought. Their condemnation of this kind of speech on public interest grounds is so powerful that it justifies lengthy quotation:

> The press is overstepping in every direction the obvious bounds of propriety and of decency. Gossip is no longer the resource of the idle and of the vicious, but has become a trade, which is pursued with industry as well as effrontery. To satisfy a prurient taste the details of sexual relations are spread broadcast in the columns of the daily papers. To occupy the indolent, column upon column is filled with idle gossip, which can only be procured by intrusion upon the domestic circle. . . . When personal gossip attains the dignity of print, and crowds the space available for matters of real interest to the community, what wonder that the ignorant and the thoughtless mistake its relative importance. Easy of comprehension, appealing to that weak side of human nature which is never wholly cast down by the misfortunes and frailties of our neighbors, no one can be surprised that it usurps the place of interest in brains capable of other things. Triviality destroys at once robustness of thought and delicacy of feelings. No enthusiasm can flourish, no generous impulse can survive under its blighting influence.[38]

Despite this powerful thesis, the Supreme Court today seems intent on ignoring the public dimension of the harmfulness of this kind of speech. The costs are regarded as exclusively private.

Together these cases seem to reveal an important feature of the Court's treatment of laws governing the press—namely, a strong disinclination to raise and address concerns about the adverse effects of some press speech on the quality of public discussion, concerns expressed at the beginning of this chapter and described in detail in reports such as that of the Hutchins commission. In only one case, *Miami Herald v. Tornillo* in 1974, has the Court even referred to such concerns. There it noted the State of Florida's argument that the circumstances of the press had changed radically since the adoption of the First Amendment: as the Hutchins report had noted, the nation had changed from a place where newspapers proliferated, and there existed an abundance of available information and opinion, to one in which a few giant organizations effectively control the marketplace of ideas.[39] Guaranteed access for persons criticized by newspapers is, the state argued, essential to quality public debate. But, though the Court took note of these concerns, it did not in the end directly address them. It simply concluded that Florida's law constituted an inappropriate "intrusion into the function of editors."

IV

Why has the Court seemingly been so oblivious to the risks to democracy of a more or less completely free press? It would be difficult to make the case that the need for active judicial review has been replaced by a system of collective press self-regulation, something the commission strongly recommended. Indeed, in the years since the commission report, there have been very few efforts in that direction. One was the creation of the National Press Council, the purpose of which was to mediate private complaints against the press. A wholly private and voluntary affair, the council eventually disbanded because several major newspapers (the New York Times among them) refused to participate on the ground that to do so would compromise their independence.[40]

The key problem has been with the Court's analytical methods. To minimize private injury inflicted by press speech is bad enough, but to treat the injury as an exclusively private matter is worse. Has the Court done this because it is ignorant of the risks?

Perhaps the Court is itself the unconscious victim of the tendency it observed in the *Sullivan* opinion about the distorting influence of our beliefs on the way we understand the world. Once it decided that the best course was to protect the press, the Court may have succumbed to the tendency Mill observed (and the Court quoted) to "argue sophistically, to suppress facts or arguments, to misstate the elements of the case, or misrepresent the opposite opinion."

One also sometimes detects in the Court's personality a kind of pathological fear of paternalism (or of being perceived as paternalistic), of confronting the possibility (as, it will be recalled, the commission did) that the problems with the press may originate with the people and that reform of the press is a means of reforming those disabilities of the larger populace. The Court is an institution that has to worry about its own legitimacy, as an unelected body deciding fundamental questions for the society. As such it is often ill-disposed to entertain arguments that this or that course of action ought to be allowed because the people are not quite all we would wish them to be. That opens the Court to charges of elitism, to which its privilege of lifetime tenure makes it especially vulnerable.

So, when the Court considers the private costs of press speech it may tend to minimize the injury, and by holding a romantic view of the public and the press it refuses to address (it privatizes) the potentially harmful impact of speech on the quality of democratic decision making.

But are these speculations sufficient to explain this seemingly self-imposed blindness to the risks to democracy of an autonomous press?

Autonomy's Control

W hen one reads the criticisms of the American press leveled by the Hutchins commission shortly after the end of the Second World War, it seems odd that the Supreme Court should spend the next four decades greatly expanding the scope of constitutional protection for the press and largely foreclosing any role for public regulation. Unless the commission overstated the press's inadequacies, or rendered an indictment of shortcomings that, though true, could be rectified by means other than public regulation, it seems strange that the Court has pursued a constitutional strategy of affording the press ever-widening autonomy. In the face of the commission's report, this modern course of constitutional law appears to reflect an immoderate judicial enthusiasm for press liberty, an unjustified extension of freedom to an unworthy recipient.

This chapter, and the next, consider the thesis that freedom of the press, as a working concept developed in the United States since the Second World War, may have been less blind to the concerns raised in Chapter 2 than one might initially assume. The present discussion initiates a study of the complex forces that may have moderated the potential risks of undesirable journalistic behavior that the autonomy principle empowers. The idea of autonomy is a complicated one, and here we shall consider the perhaps paradoxical hypothesis that inherent in the process that grants constitutional autonomy to the press is the potential for exerting a controlling and shaping influence on the way in which that autonomy, or freedom, is exercised.

I

It is best to begin with general observations about the role played by, and the kinds of influence available to, the Court through the process of constitutional adjudication. The discussion that follows focuses on the Supreme Court, but, if what is said about that Court is true, it is almost assuredly also true of the judiciary in general.

It is widely recognized that the Supreme Court possesses enormous power to affect society. We tend to think and talk about that power, however, as if it consists simply of deciding how far the other branches of federal and state government may go in controlling private behavior. Essentially, we might say, the Court is the agency that defines the scope of state authority over private behavior. Once that boundary is set, individuals may go about their business with their newly conferred freedoms, leaving the government to retreat to its remaining powers. At its best, then, the Court is seen as an impartial observer called upon to weigh competing interests and select the appropriate rules for society. Those rules, in turn, may be good or bad depending upon how well the Court understands the Constitution under which it operates and the society in which it exists.

This view of the Court, though commonly held and certainly accurate to some extent, is significantly incomplete. It overlooks the Court's profoundly important power to affect society's values while it is engaged in the process of determining society's rules. Of course, the Court resolves disputes, decides cases, applies the law. But its functions often transcend these duties. The Court does more than define the scope of governmental power. It holds an additional power, one that stems from two critical features of the process of constitutional decision making.

The first feature is the fact that we require the Court to articulate the bases for its decisions, which it does in its opinions. The second is related: because the questions presented to the Court are often central to the character of society, and because the constitutional text is largely Delphic on these questions, the Court quite naturally tends to develop a deep vision of society. Over time, at least in many areas of constitutional law, the

Court will characterize and conceptualize the social world in which we live. While these characterizations and conceptions undergird the results of particular cases, or the aggregation of results in many cases, they—and this is the critical point—may also have an impact in the world independent of those results. By articulating a vision and commenting on the nature of society, the Court is capable of shaping society's ideas about itself and hence its character.[1]

The judicial opinion, then, has a more meaningful function than the mere display of logic. It is not the legal equivalent of a mathematical proof. And that is because the Court has been assigned the task of deciding issues connected to social values. It is, literally, one of the principal speakers in the general market-place of ideas and, depending on its willingness to exercise its persuasive power, what it says contributes to the values and images citizens hold. Through the power of its speech, and as a participant in the marketplace of ideas, it can alter behavior. How that occurs, how those values and images are transmitted and embraced, may be impossible to analyze; certainly no one has done so yet. At the same time, given the high public esteem it enjoys (so high, in fact, that an exposé like *The Brethren*[2] seems to have no effect on its reputation), it would be unreasonable to proceed from a hypothesis that the Court exerts little or no such influence.

Once one recognizes the independent significance of what we might call the power of characterization inhering in the adjudication process, several aspects of that power become apparent. The most obvious is that the Court's impact may extend far beyond the realm of the official, technical, legal questions at issue in the cases it hears. As many scholars have noted, and even applauded, the Court can perform a deeply educative role in society, affecting behavior far beyond the strictly legal domain. It can, for example, address the evils of official racial discrimination and in doing so also affect public attitudes toward unofficial discrimination.

It should also be apparent that the characterization process can take on a life of its own. Like an adolescent, it may rebel against its parentally imposed function of providing reasons for decisions taken, gradually becoming an independent actor in the world of legal and public affairs. Justices at times will find it irresistible to fashion their statements with an eye toward particular behavioral effects. The content of a judicial opinion, therefore, may be better understood less as an accounting of the thought processes of the decision maker, intended simply to establish the validity of the decision, than as a deliberately constructed statement designed to exert its own influence. We now enter the realm of rhetoric.

One can also see how in a "field" of law the Court has special opportunities to exert such influence. For, as the Court returns to a particular area again and again, it not only has continuous opportunities to refine its vision but also frequent opportunities to criticize those who may fail to live up to its vision. Furthermore, each new decision may take on new and symbolic meanings, reinforcing the earlier rhetorical messages. Every new issue brought to the Court for decision will be unavoidably decided against a backdrop of related prior decisions. Within a field of law, therefore, the whole is often larger than the sum of its parts, and each new decision carries symbolic meaning that reaffirms a larger image or offers an implicit critique of the existing world if it falls short.

II

The area of freedom of the press bears the markings of this kind of judicial rhetorical influence. Certainly the process of developing a set of constitutional protections has been accompanied by the development of a *conception* of the social role of the press that is thought to justify them. And, though it was not necessary that the underlying, theoretical conception of the First Amendment embody a normative judgment about what a *good* press is, there is little doubt that that is what has occurred.

As noted in Chapter 1, the Court in *New York Times v. Sullivan* developed a general vision of the world as it set about deciding the specific issue of the degree of First Amendment protection that should be extended to defamatory statements about public officials—an undertaking it was widely praised for embracing. To answer the particular question before it, the

Court stated that it first had to reach an understanding of the general purpose of the First Amendment. This, in turn, required a set of assumptions about the nature of those who inhabit the realms of public officialdom, the pressrooms, and the public fora. Furthermore, the Court had to place these images in a context, to characterize a world relevant to the issues at hand.

Thus with *Sullivan* the Court set forth on a course—one it has followed for nearly three decades and will certainly continue to follow in the foreseeable future—of articulating an image of the press and its relation to the government and the public. We have already noted the components of that image: a government that cannot be trusted to exercise its representative powers competently or properly; a public that is incapable of gathering for itself all the information it requires to exercise its sovereign authority; and a press that performs a vital role in helping, through its powers of investigation and exposure, to reduce the risks of official incompetence and abuse, to convey information about the affairs of government, and to serve as a forum for citizens to communicate among themselves. Decision after decision has restated and refined this image of the American press.

Within this working image, the press is conceived as playing a noble, even heroic, social and political role. Significantly, the general image is suffused with ethical content: journalists should focus their attention on the political issues of the day, speak the truth about official conduct, expose errors and abuse, represent the opinions of different groups, and, of course, avoid lies and misrepresentations. The stakes are defined in very high terms indeed: a good press is a necessary condition of a good democracy. The press thus stands as the guardian and agent of the political rights of the people, and it determines the quality of public debate.

Sometimes, as occurred in *New York Times v. Sullivan,* the Court has provided extreme protection for the press, giving it the freedom to do very harmful things. But in such instances, the Court has always acknowledged that it was making bad journalism possible and, as a consequence, also made a statement about what good and bad journalism is.[3]

At other times, the Court has established constitutional protections along lines that hew more closely to the normative standard of good journalistic practice. Consider some of the constitutional doctrine surrounding libel law. In defamation suits brought by private individuals, courts now regularly determine whether the press has acted negligently, that is, not in accordance with reasonable journalistic practices.[4] Also important is the development of the distinction between private individuals and public figures. We have seen how *New York Times v. Sullivan* extended First Amendment protection to statements about public officials. For a while it appeared that this protection might cover any statement made in the course of discussions about "public issues," a position generally taken by the liberal justices.[5] In *Gertz v. Welch,* however, a conservative majority of the justices rejected that approach, saying (among other things) that it is inappropriate for the Court to distinguish between discussions of "public issues" that deserve special protections and discussions that do not.[6] The press, of course, would have been delighted if the Court had been willing to say that anything published in the press is by definition a discussion of an important public issue. Understandably, the Court found that notion unacceptable since such a ruling would effectively abolish the law of libel, something it was not prepared to do. The alternative, according to *Gertz v. Welch,* was to limit the protections extended in *New York Times v. Sullivan* to discussions about public officials and figures, the latter (as noted above) being defined primarily as individuals who have voluntarily "thrust themselves to the forefront of particular public controversies in order to influence the resolution of the issues involved."[7]

In fact, however, the retreat from a position of giving *Sullivan* protection to all discussions of "public issues" to one in which such protection applies only to discussions about "public figures" did not eliminate the need for a judicial determination of what constitutes a "public issue." That issue still adheres to the definition of a public figure ("public controversies"). *Gertz v. Welch* did not eliminate the public issue standard; it only added another element to it (voluntary participation in the controversy by the defendant). And, in *Time v. Firestone,* which involved the magazine's "milestone" report on a Palm Beach socialite involved in a racy divorce proceeding, the Court essentially decided (without acknowledging that it was) that such reportage is not the kind of "public issue or controversy" deserving of the special protections of *New York Times v. Sullivan*. The Court simply said that "[d]issolution of a marriage through judicial proceedings is not the sort of 'public controversy' referred to in *Gertz*."[8]

The point of this example is not to argue whether the Court achieved the right or wrong result in *Time v. Firestone*. The crucial observation is that in the libel area every justice on the Court has embraced a position that requires some ongoing judgment about which discussions of issues are worth special protection and which are not.[9]

A similar inquiry into the value of discussions will have to occur when the Court finally addresses the various state laws allowing recovery of damages for publication of highly embarrassing personal facts—if, that is, the Court (as I would predict) holds some of the existing law against invasions of privacy to be constitutional. All jurisdictions that allow actions for invasion of privacy extend a privilege to publication of information that is "newsworthy" or "of legitimate concern to the public."[10] This, too, requires courts to develop and articulate a set of values by which to gauge the social importance of discussions.[11] The Supreme Court will eventually institutionalize that inquiry as a constitutional matter.

Yet another Supreme Court case contributes to this gradual extension of greater protection to discussions of public issues. In *Pittsburgh Press Co. v. Pittsburgh Commission on Human Relations*,[12] the Court held that different parts of a newspaper may receive different levels of protection against regulation. The Pittsburgh Human Relations Commission had implemented an ordinance barring employment discrimination by enjoining the Pittsburgh Press from publishing Help Wanted advertisements under the headings "Jobs—Male Interest," "Jobs—Female Interest," and "Male-Female." Though the newspaper argued that its arrangement of ads under gender designations constituted "editorial judgment" protected by the First Amendment, the Court held otherwise, saying that the advertisements carried no express "position on whether, as a matter of social policy, certain positions ought to be filled by members of one or the other sex, nor does any of them criticize the Ordinance or the Commission's enforcement practices."[13]

The general point here is that, within the doctrinal structure of the First Amendment, the Court is engaged in developing and reinforcing a hierarchy of speech. Some kinds of speech are going to be deemed more worthy of constitutional protection than others because the Constitution—as interpreted by the Court—itself places a value on that discussion. Not only is the Court protecting valuable speech against government censorship or restriction but it is also proclaiming a general judgment about the kind of speech we should want in the first place. The Constitution, as so interpreted, may be changing the world while it makes rules for it, because it is simultaneously advising society about what should be valued.

The foregoing examples illustrate several ways in which the operation of the First Amendment may be creating pressures on the press to conform to certain norms of quality journalism. As the Court expands the concept of "press autonomy," it is simultaneously delineating what is unworthy of protection and public respect. Areas like libel and privacy may serve as small ports from which to launch general and at times very influential pronouncements about standards of journalism upon the sea of public debate.

III

Does the press care? Is it influenced by the identity and social role the Court enunciates for it? If so, what are the causes of that influence?

It is, as mentioned above, extremely difficult to either measure or trace the influence of law. There is survey evidence that media are increasingly aware of legal decisions and issues relating to press freedom and that most of the large press organizations have regular, first-hand experience with litigation.[14] But are journalists affected by the images of the press articulated in Supreme Court decisions? There are a number of signs that such influence exists and that it is significant.

47

The most powerful of all indicators is the simple fact that the press is dependent upon the Court for its rights. Dependency, of course, usually involves the power to help or the power to hurt; with respect to the press, the Court has both. Most important, and fundamentally, the Court has the ability to interpret the First Amendment—which is to say that it has the power to continue to apply the First Amendment as it has been applied in the past and to augment it as the press would like to see it augmented. Because it is a tacitly assumed fact of our political and constitutional life (*assumed to be such by the press at least*) that public support for a vital and vigorous doctrine of freedom of the press is forever fragile, the press is continuously conscious of the importance of having the Court ready to stand between it and the next mood of political repression. Furthermore, besides depending upon the Court for the preservation of freedoms it has already acquired, the press must also look to the Court for new accretions to its constitutional rights. Of one matter we may be certain. The press does not believe it has received all the protections it could possibly want or need under the First Amendment. The process of giving present and future meaning to the First Amendment is emphatically ongoing. The press must continuously return to the Court.[15]

It is a striking but nonetheless very real fact about Supreme Court decisions in the free press area that none provides fixed and permanent protection for the press against future government regulations. There are always caveats, conditions, and qualifications attached to decisions favorable to the press. A good example of this judicial hedging is the *Pentagon Papers* case,[16] which is widely perceived as one of the great landmark constitutional decisions in favor of the press. Though the Washington Post and the New York Times won that case, three aspects of it leave every publisher wondering—even after that spectacular victory—whether he or she will win in the next national security case. First, the legal principle applied by the justices in the case was not absolute. It depended on judicial review of the facts, and in particular on the degree of harm that could reasonably be foreseen from publication of the papers.[17] The next set of government documents may be considered more harmful, and it will, in any event, be difficult to compare them to the Pentagon Papers to know whether and how much they are. Second, a major premise of the government's decision was a strong presumption of the invalidity of prior restraints—which in the *Pentagon Papers* case involved an *injunction* sought against future publication. Several justices noted the possibility that the ruling was inapplicable to subsequent punishments, a legal term that refers to legal actions initiated after publication.[18] Third, several justices observed, with seemingly pregnant meaning, that an injunction was improper because Congress had not enacted a statute authorizing such judicial action,[19] thereby raising the possibility that if Congress did enact such a statute even an injunction would be constitutional.[20]

These uncertainties about the holding of *Pentagon Papers* are not uncommon even among major free press decisions. Similar caveats occur in all of the cases surveyed in Chapter 1.

As a result of all these conditions, the press has a compelling self-interest in meeting the Court's expectations about its role in society. This motive supplements other, less self-interested or instrumental reasons why the press might choose to look to the Court for guidance about its identity. The press may even follow the Court's directives out of simple respect, as many members of society apparently do. It is hard to support a claim for that kind of influence, however, and we need not rely on it when the powerful motivation of self-interest is involved.

We can, on the other hand, expand on this general conception of the power of the Court to affect the condition of the press in society, and, through that power, to influence press behavior. The Court's influence over public opinion is yet another source of potential constraint, for, as much as any institution in society, the press must attend to public opinion. Because it operates in a market, peoples' preferences will ultimately prevail. Expectations about the press are reflected in market choices, and, because public opinion is obviously related to the imposition of legal controls, the press has to be concerned about hostile or antagonistic public opinion as it ponders the security of its constitutional freedoms. If the public is unhappy with the press, constitutionally allowed sanctions may well be imposed. What is constitutionally prohibited may nonetheless be tried, causing aggravation for the press until it can be remedied—or, worse, seep disguised and undetected through the cracks of constitutionally permissible regulation. It is, for example, a common, and I suspect accurate, lament of the press that juries in libel cases often issue damage awards to plaintiffs out of desire to punish the press for perceived general misbehavior.[21]

There are many indications that the press pays close attention to the ways in which the Court and the public understand the risks of an unregulated press. Sensing that, psychologically, a concrete instance of abuse can have disproportionately strong gravitational effects on judgments about the risks of press freedom, the institution is sometimes quick to condemn what it perceives to be misbehavior by one or more of its members that will reflect poorly on the press as a whole (creating, in other words, an adverse "central image"). A dramatic illustration of this tendency occurred a few years after the press victory in *Pentagon Papers* when a magazine called the Progressive announced its intention to publish an article describing the construction of a hydrogen bomb. The Progressive claimed that all of its information had been gathered from public sources, which was to be the point of the story. It further argued that *Pentagon Papers* protected its right to publish the article. The government challenged this claim and filed suit for an injunction against publication, asserting (with affidavits from members of the cabinet and the scientific community) that if this article were published terrorist nations would be significantly aided in developing the hydrogen bomb.[22]

The reaction to the Progressive's plan by the established press, including the New York Times and the Washington Post, was swift and severely critical.[23] The criticisms were of several kinds but at root there seemed to be an understandable fear within the press that bad cases make bad law. It seemed widely feared that the sensational victory of *Pentagon Papers* would be put in jeopardy if the Progressive asserted its constitutional right to publish an article that appeared to be the real-life version of a professor's final, clinching hypothetical as she set about offering a devastating parade of horribles about the nightmarish implications of *Pentagon Papers*.

The press's concern reflects a widely shared intuition about the nature of decision making, a phenomenon that manifests itself in many contexts. We have already noted how every lawyer knows the significance of having an appealing case with which to advance a general legal proposition. Harry Kalven acutely observed, as he assessed the significance of *New York Times v. Sullivan* to the development of First Amendment theory, how blacks in the civil rights movement steadily regained First Amendment territory that had been lost in the prior decade by socially feared Communists.[24] But we also think by images more generally, and the nature of our lives is affected by the experiential images we hold in our minds. Thus, Alexander Bickel, who represented the New York Times in *Pentagon Papers,* later mused that, even though the principle of freedom of the press emerged victorious in the end, our sense of freedom suffered a loss simply because the government violated the virginity of the principle by taking the extraordinary step of seeking to enjoin the press from publishing these documents.[25] In the face of this concrete instance of a government effort to silence the press, Bickel suggested that we could never again entertain, with conviction, the pleasurable image of an unbounded, if unused, freedom. And so it would be, it seemed, from the opposite direction with the *Progressive* case: In the future the risks of a free press would be more vividly imagined, more heavily felt, every time we addressed the principle of freedom of the press.

In the *Progressive* case the government prevailed in federal district court, and an injunction was issued. Not surprisingly, the trial judge refused to assume the burden of protecting speech at a potential cost of nuclear annihilation.[26] Before the decision could be appealed, however, another newspaper obtained the article and published it. With the facts out, the government abandoned its lawsuit against the Progressive. By this time, it was becoming clear that the projected harm from publication had been grossly inflated by the government. The press rather abashedly, and belatedly, rallied in support of the Progressive.[27] Apart from the question whether the press responded either appropriately or admirably in this particular case, the episode still stands as an example of how the press polices itself in order to preserve its constitutional image.

If the *Progressive* case illustrates, if only anecdotally, the willingness of the press to censure what it perceives as journalistic abuses, on a larger scale its reaction to the Burger Court decisions in the free press area partially illustrates its concern with the power of the judiciary to sanction or injure it through what the Court writes in its opinions. This requires us to think more deeply about the relationship between the press and the Court.

It is not fanciful to see *New York Times v. Sullivan* as establishing a special bond between the Court and the press. With that opinion the Court seemed eager to take on the role of constitutional advocate for, as well as protector of, the press. Of course, the Court had its own reasons for proposing such a relationship. The New York Times was, after all, being punished by a Southern jury for supporting the very civil rights movement the Court had fostered and was enforcing. Nor is it far-fetched to view the real intended victim in that case as the Supreme Court itself, with the New York Times serving simply as its surrogate. But a sensitive understanding of the two institutions, the Court and the press, may yield other, more subtle explanations for the sense of solidarity between them. Something in the identities of both institutions may lead naturally to such a bond. They share the condition of standing, as it were, at the margin of society. Both function as social critics. Neither possesses the powers of enforcement held by the legislative and executive branches, though each is said to be a "branch" with major governmental responsibilities. Both are regularly attacked for assuming powers unconferred by the representative process. They exist in the ever-awkward position of having a grand role to perform without being electorally authorized, democratically legitimated, to perform that role. The two institutions, therefore, may have a kind of natural, institutional affinity arising from their shared social role and status—all of it, of course, reinforced by the press's many good reasons for not wanting to cross the Court.

As the era of the Warren Court gave way to the era of the Burger Court, however, an important change occurred in the character of this complex relationship. From the press there soon emerged expressions of consternation and criticism of the new Court.[28] By their severity, one would suppose that the press had suddenly lost significant cases before the Court. The press did lose some cases, but very few were significant. In fact, during this period of history the press, by any measure, gained far more constitutional ground than it lost. Among what are today regarded as the most significant free press decisions many come from the Burger Court era.[29] Yet the press regularly lamented the performance of that Court, so much so that even some of the liberal justices broke their traditional vow of silence on decided cases and expressed their dissatisfaction, even amazement, at the criticism.[30]

The best way to make sense of this decade or more of strained relations is to begin with an understanding of the Court as having a dual capacity to decide the scope of the constitutional freedom available to the press and to characterize and shape society's attitudes toward it as a social institution. What the Burger Court did, and the Warren Court did not, was introduce in its opinions a tone of skepticism, and even outright criticism, regarding the American press. At times this produced opinions that appear schizophrenic. The most prominent is *Miami Herald v. Tornillo,* the 1974 decision that struck down a Florida statute mandating a right of reply for political candidates criticized by newspapers. It may be recalled that the opening discussion in the majority opinion contained an extended critique of the modern press, portraying it as a monopolistic "big business" with the "capacity to manipulate popular opinions and change the course of events."[31] The text and footnotes of the Court's opinion are sprinkled with data about the twin phenomena of increasing chain ownership and one-newspaper cities, and for the interested reader there are several references to articles and books that elaborate on this general indictment. All this is offered to support the view that "vast changes" have placed "in a few hands the power to inform the American people and shape public opinion."[32]

Then the text suddenly shifts its tone and concludes with an emphatic rejection of the use of legal controls to correct this unhappy situation. "However much validity may be found in these arguments," the Court says of its foregoing criticisms, "at each point the implementation of a remedy such as an enforceable right of access necessarily calls for some mechanism, either governmental or consensual. If it is governmental coercion, this at once brings about a confrontation with the express provisions of the First Amendment and the judicial gloss on that Amendment developed over the years."[33] In this contest, the Court concludes, the First Amendment must win.

By the end of the opinion, the reader is left, significantly, with an ambiguous message: either the Court is continuing, in the tradition of *Sullivan,* to stand by the press as an institution richly deserving of its First Amendment rights, or, in the vein of the Hutchins commission report, it is endorsing the view that the overall performance of the press is alarmingly deficient, actually on the brink of losing its constitutional freedoms.[34]

Another example of the judicial subtext of criticism, even hostility, in the Burger Court press cases is the 1972 decision in *Branzburg v. Hayes.*[35] The Court rejected a claim by the press for a qualified privilege not to reveal to a grand jury information a reporter had obtained from a confidential source, including the identity of the source. Though *Branzburg* was decided against the press, equally disturbing from its standpoint was the unenthusiastic characterization of the press in Justice White's opinion for the Court. It was possible to reject a reporter's privilege on the ground that it would be against the interests of the press; many within the press opposed the idea. But the Court took a different view. In a 1977 article, Vincent Blasi astutely noted how Justice White "characterized the press as a private-interest group rather than an institution with a central function to perform in the constitutional system of checks and balances."[36] White "labeled the source relationships that the reporters sought to maintain 'a private system of informers operated by the press to report on criminal conduct' [cautioning] that this system would be 'unaccountable to the public' were a reporter's privilege to be recognized."[37] This was a far cry from the traditional Fourth Estate image of the press, and of a piece with other signals that the press was not held by the Burger Court in the high regard it had enjoyed under the Warren Court.[38]

All this may well have served to legitimate the storm of public criticism that gathered around the press during this time.[39] That, I suspect, was precisely what the press sensed and what came to underlay its resentment toward the Burger Court. If true, it is indicative of press sensitivity to the way it is portrayed in the Court's opinions.

IV

The primary focus of this analysis has thus far been on the control of journalistic abuses. But there are broader implications which also should be made explicit. When the Court attempts to shape the manner in which the press exercises the liberty afforded to it under the First Amendment, it may seek either a narrow or a broad influence. A narrow influence would involve indication of the outer parameters of ethical journalistic behavior. The desire for broad influence, on the other hand, could lead the Court to try to shape the whole character of the press. Then, the Court could use both the results of particular cases and the rhetoric of its opinions to inspire a particular kind of press, not just to identify and establish a floor of proper behavior. In fact, much that has occurred under the journalistic autonomy approach to the First Amendment—and much that seems strange—can be understood as a broad effort to shape the type of press we will have.

Seen in this context, the Supreme Court's press decisions resonate with a world in which the press is seeking an identity. There are many different styles of press. Some societies may expect the press to be loyal to the government and help maintain social stability by avoiding criticisms that would undermine it. This is the press of present-day Singapore or Taiwan. At the other extreme, a society may want a press conceived in the image of the artist, one who lives (figuratively) outside society, beyond normal conventions, and who is therefore better able to see and expose its shortcomings. America's conception of the press tends to lean in that direction, though it is an image blurred. The model of journalistic autonomy, embodied in the constitutional idea of freedom of the press, breathes life into that image.

One must, however, begin with an appreciation of the tremendous pressures within society and the press against such a vision being realized. The spirit of intellectual independence is not easy to come by or keep. There always exist nearly irresistible pressures not to report things as they are; it is frequently easier to report things as people (and especially advertisers) wish them to be. Anyone whose life work it is to report on the day's events will inevitably experience the potentially crushing power of conformity. One need only remember the fate of Socrates. Surely all the newspapers in the country, especially those known as "community newspapers," struggle daily with the risk of becoming an organ of the local chamber of commerce. What is reported makes a real difference in peoples' lives, and when that happens life will not be simple for those thought to be responsible. The costs of exposing official corruption or of communicating unpleasant truths or the labors of fully considering complex social issues are often great; the simpler, more lucrative path is to provide simplicities and entertainment. It is easy to perform badly.[40]

For the principle of journalistic autonomy, this means several things.

First, the Court sometimes perceives itself, and reasonably so, as an advocate for a free press. In a world in which powerful pressures operate to stifle an independent press, the Court's voice must be strong and forceful. The general urging his troops into battle does not offer qualified and balanced pronouncements on the risks ahead but inspires them with visions of glory. The parent of a timid child does not stress the possibility of failure but says he can be anything he wants to be. The Court, too, becomes a natural enthusiast for the press and its independence. This means it will, as it does, understate the costs of press freedom. It also means that its opinions will often carry the tone of paeans to the benefits of such liberty. Even justices who usually elect the prosaic over the passionate become eloquent in this area of the law. Justice White in *Miami Herald v. Tornillo* spoke of "the virtually insurmountable barrier between government and the print media," of how we are "intensely skeptical about those measures that would allow government to insinuate itself into the editorial rooms of this Nation's press,"[41] and of "the elementary First Amendment proposition that government may not force a newspaper to print copy which, in its journalistic discretion, it chooses to leave on the newsroom floor."[42] In this passion he is representative.[43]

The results of cases are also part and parcel of this enterprise of creating a social identity for the press, for the autonomy thus conferred has its own rhetorical meaning. Autonomy generally means the freedom to make mistakes. Its use is widespread, in business, universities, and families. Its rationality is composed of several elements. Typically, we say that autonomy is conferred when a person with power to intervene has inferior expertise or biases that distort his or her ability to exercise that power. But that cannot be the whole of it. It cannot be a simple judgment about relative capacity. Also inhering in the conferral of autonomy is the implicit recognition of the dignity and capacity of the newly autonomous. It is an extension of trust. And, whether it is worthy praise or insidious flattery, it can change the person to whom the power to err is extended.

This means that the extremes of protection afforded the press under the journalistic autonomy model may also serve as a metaphor for an intellectual style. To deny state regulation of the press, to declare it "unaccountable" to official authority, is to emphasize its intellectual independence from every constraint, including that of the market. Constitutional autonomy feeds the universal wish to adopt a posture toward the world that says, in effect, no one will tell you what to do. It taps, as it were, into a personality trait that alters behavior.

Much of what happens under the journalistic autonomy model, therefore, can only be understood in psychological terms, or, if that sounds too clinical, in terms of shaping identity. In other words, the reasons for overprotection of the press are not so much the ones given by *New York Times v. Sullivan*— that it is necessary because the government cannot be trusted, because human mistakes are inevitable, or because fear of litigation leads to timidity—but the idea that the removal of a superior, supervising authority contributes to the creation of a spirit of intellectual independence.

There is, however, some uncertainty within the journalistic autonomy model, and within the press itself, about the desired identity of the press. Our vision is slightly blurred. Two images compete for power. The dominant image of the press, since *Sullivan,* has emphasized its institutional role. This image views the press as the Fourth Estate, as an entity serving a critical quasi-official function in the political system.[44] It elevates the press to the highest rung on society's organizational chart and anoints it as the public's representative. The rhetorical advantages of this image are self-evident. It is, as noted earlier, suffused with ethical content. It is also instrumental in persuading others to accept extensions of press freedom because the claim can be made that society as a whole is better off for it. But psychologically this image is troublesome to many. There are three concerns, each working in different directions. One is the fear that the press will become *too aggressive* in its conception of itself as the knight-errant of the public. It may, in its investigative activities, for example, assume the role of public prosecutor but do great injury due to lack of training or because it is unconstrained by the other principles of the Bill of Rights. The second concern is that the press will become too "official," and, therefore, too bland and institutional, in its outlook and performance. There is always the danger that it will become too much a part of the establishment it is meant to watch. It is also feared that the public, having come to think of the press as an institutional organ, will tend to impose additional burdens upon it. With privilege comes responsibility, it might be thought.[45]

All these concerns underlay opposition to the press's claim in *Branzburg,* for example, that reporters have a constitutionally based privilege not to testify before grand juries.[46] In fact, they arise whenever the press seeks special First Amendment status or rights, as it has on occasion in the newsgathering area.[47] And they arise more broadly—often in discussions about the nature and function of journalism schools—whenever journalism is described as a "profession," like medicine or law.[48] The fears, ultimately, involve identity and questions about how the press will behave and be viewed if a particular legal rule or rationale is adopted.

Stimulating and reinforcing this sense of independent-mindedness is the function, intended or not, of another major branch of the theory-qua-identity of the press. Frequently it is associated with the rhetoric of rights: the press is said to have the "right" to report what it wishes, irrespective of the harm this may cause or whether society as a whole is better off for it.[49] There is, of course, a deep and rich debate over the question whether rights exist to serve the public good or for some other reason. Much of it revolves around the scope of human behavior allowable under each theory. But there is also a psychological, a rhetorical, dimension to the use of the language of rights in political discourse. It can be a means of stimulating rebelliousness toward authority. It can encourage an attitude, a posture. The Hutchins commission seemed to recognize this process. At one point the report speaks of the "historical work" that a simple rights-oriented approach to freedom of the press had performed. There are "no unconditional rights," it tells us, although the "notion of rights, costless, unconditional, conferred by the Creator at birth, was a marvelous fighting principle against arbitrary governments and had its historical work to do." Now, in a "context of an achieved political freedom," the need for limits "becomes evident." For the commission the problem was also one of the identity created by the rhetoric of "theory": "The unworkable and invalid conception of birthrights, wholly divorced from the condition of duty, has tended to beget an arrogant type of individualism which makes a mockery of every free institution, including the press."[50]

But such an intellectual style may not be all bad. To emphasize that the press is neither professional nor official, but independent and unaccountable to the ordinary calculations of the public good, can be profitably stimulating to journalism. The image of the reporter-as-Ulysses has its appeal *and* its social function—even if it is described as the antithesis of a social function. Consider, for example, the attitude one takes toward one's own beliefs. Part of the image of the press under study here stresses the value of commitment to one's beliefs—one of the threads, it will be recalled, of the *Sullivan* analysis.[51] Just as the lawyer in the adversarial process is told to make a wholehearted intellectual commitment to his or her client's position, so the press is told to give full voice to their positions. As a matter of theory about human nature and the paths to truth, such a system can make sense—a zealous advocate sometimes has the advantage of discovery denied to the balanced and fair-minded.

V

The deeper we probe into the First Amendment jurisprudence of freedom of the press, and into the journalistic autonomy model, the more profoundly important and complex becomes the process by which that model is given effect. What appear on the surface to be theoretical justifications of the First Amendment become, on further inspection, rhetorical stimulants designed to inspire the press to particular behavior and to limit abuses from the freedom conferred.

Whether judicial rhetoric in the First Amendment area makes a difference in the practical world of journalism cannot be conclusively established. Certainly, the best work on the sociology of the press identifies the 1960s as a time of profound changes within the American press. That was a time when the press became increasingly suspicious of, and antagonistic toward, the government. It initiated the era of the "new journalism" and a radical critique of the traditional notions of objectivity in reporting. Distrust of the official versions of the world became a firmly held, working premise. To sociologists of journalism these crises of identity stemmed from the widespread feeling within the press that the government was increasingly bent on, at best, managing the news, or, at worst, manipulating the news; and from the fact that the press was situated in a society with a growing antigovernment, antiestablishment, political sentiment.[52] But, just as those in law tend to pay too much attention to the results of judicial decisions and too little to the ways in which the legal process influences attitudes and values within the broader society, so those who study the behavioral developments within the press have paid too little attention to the effects of law on those developments. It would seem that, at the very least, the extremely close resonance between the themes of *New York Times v. Sullivan* and its successors (especially the antiseditious libel imagery) and the changes in the identity, and ethos, of journalism at the same time ought to make us alert to the potential for a causal connection.

Here, then, is the proposition: the evolution of press liberty over the last four decades, in the wake of the Hutchins commission report, has meant far more than the extension of liberty. It has also involved the emergence of a prestigious social institution—the Court—that helps to define and create a kind of press.

As it goes about its business, the Court is continually creating images of what American journalism is and of what it should be. Those images may have bite.[53] And, if they do, it is important to understand that the Court is addressing a larger reality than the technical legal issues placed before it, year after year, for decision.

CHAPTER FOUR

The Secondary Image

I n fact, we have never had a simple system of an autonomous press in this country, neither in the form discussed in the first chapter nor as reinterpreted in the third chapter. The American experience of freedom of the press, during most of this century, has included extensive government intervention through a regulatory system designed and implemented precisely to deal with many of the problems raised in Chapter 2. The intention in this chapter is to describe that experience. In Chapter 5 we will consider its potential significance for the system as a whole and the concept of press autonomy in particular.

To this point in the discussion, in the course of speaking about the "press," there has been little mention of the electronic media of television or radio. Few readers probably detected that omission. The very typicality of such an oversight, however, is at the essence of the remarkably complex system of freedom of the press in twentieth-century America.

For six decades now, there has been extensive regulation of broadcasting. If "press" is defined as those primary institutions that convey information and ideas about public issues to large numbers of people, then surely the broadcast media must be included. Yet, psychologically, this country has neglected to incorporate into its notions about freedom of the press the facts that the broadcast media are highly regulated and that they are an integral part of the American "press." In the opening chapter, I asked readers to consider how they would briefly describe the concept of freedom of the press in America. I have little doubt that most would answer with an image of the print media in mind. Most would say that in this society government is forbidden to license and regulate the content of the press except in the most unusual and clearly delineated circumstances. It is assumed that we rely on the market, not the government, to regulate what is supplied by the press. And we say this despite an extensive regulatory system that covers, figuratively if not literally, half the press—a system that involves both licensing and regulation of content.

I

In previous chapters we have considered a variety of concerns one might have about an unregulated press, and we have further considered how the journalistic autonomy model might, in its own way, be responsive to such concerns. I now want to examine how the broadcast regulatory system, which has existed since the Radio Act of 1927,[1] responds to identical concerns in a fundamentally different manner.

The American system of broadcast regulation has been built on two phenomena: a fear of the power of television and radio to control the content of public discussion, and a concomitant belief in the inability of the market to adequately control that power. Under the most general mandate imaginable, the Communications Act of 1934 (the sequel legislation to the 1927 Radio Act)[2] created the Federal Communications Commission and vested it with the authority to regulate this new electronic medium as the "public interest, convenience or necessity" demands.[3] Although section 326 specifically denies the commission the power of "censorship,"[4] this prohibition has not excluded all public regulation of content.

Public controls begin with a government-issued license. Applicants competing for spectrum space must indicate what they intend to say, albeit in a general way, in order to have a chance of being awarded a license to operate. For years the commission warned would-be broadcasters that to be successful in the licensing process the applicant had to promise to spend some time covering public issues and local affairs.[5] And, since licenses are granted for limited periods of time, the successful applicant's promises and performance could be evaluated and compared to competing applications at the license renewal stage.

More important, those who are fortunate enough to obtain licenses—which in general have been extraordinarily lucrative—must abide by various rules regarding discussion of public issues. The best known of these strictures are the fairness doctrine and the equal time rule. Under the fairness doctrine, broadcasters have two primary obligations. First, they are required to spend a reasonable amount of time covering "controversial issues of public importance," and are thereby prohibited from airing entertainment programming exclusively. Second, broadcasters, when covering controversial issues of public importance, must be fair and balanced in the presentation of opposing viewpoints.[6]

In the 1960s, the commission decided that the fairness doctrine should have two more specific, subsidiary rules. The first is the so-called personal attack rule, under which any individual or group whose "honesty, character, integrity or like personal qualities" are attacked during the discussion of a controversial issue of public importance must be so notified by the broadcaster and afforded "a reasonable opportunity to respond over the licensee's facilities."[7] In light of my earlier criticism of the Supreme Court's decision in *New York Times v. Sullivan,* in which the cost of defamatory statements to the quality of public discussion was not considered, it is worth noting that the explicit purpose behind the personal attack rule was not to provide a method of rehabilitating the private reputations of defamed individuals. Rather, its purpose was to insure that public discussion is as accurate as possible. The best way to achieve this level of accuracy, the rule assumes, is to provide an opportunity to speak for those who have the greatest interest in presenting the opposing viewpoint.

The second subsidiary rule is the "political editorializing rule," under which any broadcaster who in an "editorial" endorses or opposes a candidate for public office must notify the other candidates and offer them a "reasonable opportunity" to respond.[8] This, too, was designed to insure dissemination of complete information to the public.

The Communications Act itself rarely approaches the specific, and rules such as the fairness doctrine emerged through the commission's power to advance the "public convenience, interest, and necessity." The equal time rule, on the other hand, was part of the statute from the beginning, incorporated in section 315.[9] With some exceptions, it provides that, whenever "any licensee shall permit any person who is a legally qualified candidate for any public office to use a broadcasting station, he shall afford equal opportunities to all other such candidates for that office in the use of such broadcasting station."[10] In 1972 Congress added another specific rule to this general family of regulations. Known as the "reasonable access" rule, it allows the commission to revoke a license "for willful or repeated failure to allow reasonable access to, or to permit purchase of, reasonable amounts of time for the use of a broadcasting station by a legally qualified candidate for Federal elective office on behalf of his candidacy."[11]

Together, these rules and doctrines have provided the primary sources of public regulation, or control, over the content of what is published over the airwaves, all of them seeking to improve the quality of public debate of public issues. Three additional kinds of regulation might be noted.

The commission has a policy of prohibiting broadcasters from deliberately "distorting" the news it purports to cover. "Rigging or slanting the news is a most heinous act against the public interest," the commission said in 1969, and promised in "all cases where we may appropriately do so, we shall act to protect the public interest in this important respect."[12] That case involved a CBS documentary, "Hunger in America," in which an infant was presented as if suffering from malnutrition when it was actually afflicted with a different disease.

The commission also has exercised control over the use of "indecent" material in broadcast programming. It has done this with the sanction of the Supreme Court, despite the fact that the same degree of regulation would not be constitutionally permissible if applied to the print media. Acting under the authority of a separate statute prohibiting "indecent" material on the airwaves, the commission has, for example, placed a letter of censure in a radio station's license file for airing a monologue by a well-known comedian about the curious social attitudes toward four-letter words.[13]

Finally, in an effort to maintain diversity of programming

within communities, the commission has at times exercised control over format changes by radio stations—in cases, for example, when a station has sought to abandon a classical program in order to become yet another rock station.[14]

II

To begin to put some flesh and blood on these bones of broadcast regulation, I want first to discuss how the Supreme Court has responded to it. A major part of the broadcast media regulation experience in this country has involved the interaction between the courts, especially the Supreme Court, and the commission. There can be little question that the Supreme Court has provided (as it almost always does) the most visible articulation of what the broadcast regulatory enterprise is all about. Through its decisions it has both shaped and defined the experience.

One of the most stiking features of the Court's performance has been the way it has conceived of the enterprise in First Amendment terms. Nothing less has been involved than a complete conceptual reordering of the relationships between the government, the press, and the public that was established with *New York Times v. Sullivan*.

One must begin with an understanding of how the Supreme Court has responded to First Amendment challenges to the broadcast regulatory system. It did so on a theory that broadcasting is "different" from other media, and hence can be regulated not with impunity but in a manner consistent with the "public interest" in healthy debate.

Though the earliest legislation on broadcast regulation was enacted in 1927, the Court did not consider a First Amendment challenge to it until 1943. That case was *National Broadcasting Co. v. United States*,[15] and it involved a complicated set of regulations known as the "chain broadcasting" rules, which sought in various ways to limit the dominance of networks over individual station licensees. Just as the Court seems to have tried to stimulate the independence of the print media (through both results and opinions), so has the commission waged a life-long, if not wholly successful, campaign to encourage local broadcasters to remain independent of the homogenizing grip of the national networks. Through the "chain broadcasting" rules, the commission imposed limits on the degree of autonomy a licensee could give up when joining a network.[16] Important as the issue of the statutory validity of these regulations was, in the long run the constitutional issue—and the Court's disposition of it—was of far greater significance.

NBC raised a First Amendment objection to the regulatory system as a whole and to the particular rule in this case. The Court treated the claim as nearly frivolous, dismissing it briefly at the end of a long opinion. Justice Frankfurter, its author, spoke in words that have been repeated frequently whenever the issue of the legitimacy of broadcast regulation has been challenged. Because more people want to broadcast than there is room to accommodate them in the electromagnetic spectrum, he said, and available space must be allocated, the government was the most reasonable body to perform that allocation. While the government should not choose among competing applicants on the basis of the political preferences of the commissioners, it seemed equally obvious to the Court that the government should be afforded a wide berth in assigning and regulating the use of frequencies according to its vision of the "public convenience, interest and necessity." Below is the full text of Justice Frankfurter's remarks on the First Amendment issue of broadcast regulation:

We come, finally, to an appeal to the First Amendment. The Regulations, even if valid in all other respects, must fall because they abridge, say the appellants, their right of free speech. If that be so, it would follow that every person whose application for a license to operate a station is denied by the Commission is thereby denied his constitutional right of free speech. Freedom of utterance is abridged to many who wish to use the limited facilities of radio. Unlike other modes of expression, radio inherently is not available to all. That is its unique characteristic, and that is why, unlike other modes of expression, it is subject to governmental regulation. Because it cannot be used by all, some who wish to use it must be denied. But Congress did not authorize the Commission to choose among applicants upon the basis of their political, economic or social views, or upon any other capricious basis. If it did, or if the Commission by these Regulations proposed a choice among applicants upon some such basis, the issue before us would be wholly different. The question here is simply whether the Commission, by announcing that it will refuse licenses to persons who engage in specified network practices (a basis for choice which we hold is comprehended within the statutory criterion of "public interest"), is thereby denying such persons the constitutional right of free speech. The right of free speech does not include, however, the right to use the facilities of radio without a license. The licensing system established by Congress in the Communications Act of 1934 was a proper exercise of its power over commerce. The standard it provided for the licensing of stations was the "public interest, convenience, or necessity." Denial of a station license on that ground, if valid under the Act, is not a denial of free speech.[17]

For several decades this statement has stood as the authoritative pronouncement on the question of the constitutionality of broadcast regulation, and it has become known as the "scarcity rationale."

Twenty-seven years later the Court returned to the question of the First Amendment and broadcast regulation, doing so in the context of a claim by a radio station that the fairness doctrine was unconstitutional. A small station in Pennsylvania had aired a commentary by the Reverend Billy James Hargis, during which Hargis attacked Fred J. Cook, the author of a book, *Goldwater: Extremist on the Right.* Hargis claimed that Cook "had been fired by a newspaper for making false charges against city officials; that Cook had then worked for a Communist-affiliated publication; that he had defended Alger Hiss and attacked J. Edgar Hoover and the Central Intelligence Agency; and that he had now written a 'book to smear and destroy Barry Goldwater,'"[18] In fact, as Professor Fred Friendly of the Columbia School of Journalism was to discover years later,[19] Cook had been supported in the writing of the book by the

Democratic National Committee. The committee also made it a practice of monitoring conservative, right-wing broadcasts and of ensuring that fairness doctrine complaints were filed whenever conservative positions were aired. When this monitoring process brought the Hargis broadcast to its attention, Cook was instructed to file a complaint under the personal attack rule and demand free time to reply. When the station refused, Cook took his complaint to the FCC, which ruled in his favor. The station appealed that decision to the Court of Appeals for the District of Columbia, which affirmed the commission rule. The Supreme Court granted certiorari, and the result, a unanimous decision in *Red Lion Broadcasting Co. v. Federal Communications Commission*,[20] was an opinion that was to broadcast regulation what *New York Times v. Sullivan* was to the principle of journalistic autonomy.

In *Red Lion,* the Court reaffirmed the scarcity rationale that Justice Frankfurter had enunciated in the *NBC* case nearly three decades earlier. As before, the broadcasters made a sweeping claim of unconstitutionality: "The broadcasters challenge the fairness doctrine and its specific manifestations in the personal attack and political editorial rules on conventional First Amendment grounds, alleging that the rules abridge their freedom of speech and press. Their contention is that the First Amendment protects their desire to use their allotted frequencies continuously to broadcast whatever they choose, and to exclude whomever they choose from ever using that frequency. No man may be prevented from saying or publishing what he thinks, or from refusing in his speech or other utterances to give equal weight to the views of his opponents. This right, they say, applies equally to broadcasters."[21]

Recognizing that "broadcasting is clearly a medium affected by a First Amendment interest," the Court proceeded on the assumption that "differences in the characteristics of new media justify differences in the First Amendment standards applied to them."[22] Noise restrictions on the use of voice amplifying equipment, for example, were necessary and permissible so that some speech does not "snuff out the free speech of others."[23] With broadcasting there was also a difference, which lay in the fact that "only a tiny fraction of those with resources and intelligence can hope to communicate by radio at the same time if intelligible communication is to be had, even if the entire radio spectrum is utilized in the present state of commercially acceptable technology."[24] Because of the inherent physical limitation on the number of usable frequencies, the government had the responsibility "to tell some applicants that they could not broadcast at all because there was room for only a few."[25] Under these circumstances, "[w]here there are substantially more individuals who want to broadcast than there are frequencies to allocate, it is idle to posit an unabridgeable First Amendment right to broadcast comparable to the right of every individual to speak, write, or publish."[26] The Court went on to conclude: "There is nothing in the First Amendment which prevents the Government from requiring a licensee to share his frequency with others and to conduct himself as a proxy or fiduciary with obligations to present those views and voices which are representative of his community and which would otherwise, by necessity, be barred from the airwaves."[27]

Cases subsequent to *Red Lion* have reaffirmed this general approach to broadcast regulation. Four years later, the Court decided another important case in *Columbia Broadcasting System, Inc. v. Democratic National Committee*.[28] In that decision, a majority of the Court rejected a claim by two political groups (the Democratic National Committee and the Business Executives' Move for Vietnam Peace) that both the Communications Act and the First Amendment mandated that the commission require broadcasters to accept paid advertisements on public issues when proffered by "responsible" individuals and groups. According to the majority, it was sensible and acceptable for Congress to have decided that the power of selecting what was worthy of presentation in the media resides with the broadcasters and not with private individuals (who are certainly not invariably "'the best judge' of what the listening public ought to hear or indeed the best judge of the merits of his or her views").[29] Broadcasters, said the majority, are subject to public oversight by the commission and operate under the aegis of the fairness doctrine. The dissenters—Justices Brennan and Marshall—would have found a statutory and constitutional right of access on the part of individual members of the public to purchase airtime.[30]

Finally, in 1981 in *Columbia Broadcasting System, Inc. v. FCC*,[31] the Court upheld the reasonable access rule of section 312(a)(7), requiring broadcasters to provide candidates for federal elective office reasonable opportunities to purchase airtime to present their candidacies. The Court repeated the scarcity rationale of *Red Lion,* but it also referred to a rationale that had arisen frequently in general discussions about the legitimacy of broadcast regulation. That is the fact that broadcasting makes use of a "publicly owned resource" and can, therefore, be publicly controlled in the manner of its use: "A licensed broadcaster is 'granted the free and exclusive use of a limited and valuable part of the public domain; when he accepts that franchise it is burdened by enforceable public obligations.'"[32] Following the logic of the public domain thesis, the Court concluded that this particular statutory access requirement "represents an effort by Congress to assure that an important resource—the airwaves—will be used in the public interest."[33]

Before closing this review of Supreme Court decisions on broadcast regulation, I want to draw attention to their most striking feature, which is not the Court's holdings as such. It is rather the Court's virtual celebration of public regulation.

To appreciate fully the significance of these decisions, one must distinguish between the Court's efforts to identify a material difference between the electronic and the print media that would justify the differential treatment of them in matters of public policy and constitutional theory; and the Court's *attitude* toward, or *conception* of, freedom of the press in the context of the broadcast media, compared with the Court's attitude toward freedom of the press in the context of the print media.

With regard to the latter issue, it is helpful first to consider not what the Court's attitude in *Red Lion* was but what it might have been. In the era following *New York Times v. Sullivan,* the time during which *Red Lion* was heard, one might have expected the Court to say something like the following: There is a deeply rooted principle in this society, reflected in the First Amendment to the Constitution, that the press shall be free and unregulated. The press may abuse that freedom, but this is a risk we take because we fear that, to give government the power to control the press, even for the best of ends, is also to give government the power of censorship for the worst of ends. In the matter of broadcasting, however, circumstances compel us to see the limit of that principle and to permit some government intervention. We allow this reluctantly, however, with every intention of being cautiously tolerant toward government control and with every intention of seeing that the broadcast media revert to the company of their fellow print media journalists as quickly as the circumstances that impelled their departure can be eliminated, or are demonstrated to have been illogical or illusory.

This, however, was not even close to the Court's attitude toward broadcast regulation. On the contrary, it enthusiastically embraced the concept of regulation. It took the affirmative and reconceived the fundamental theoretical underpinnings of this vision of the relationship between the press and the government, and never said a word about the print media analogy or the historical fear of government oversight of the press. To read the Court's unanimous opinion in *Red Lion* is to step into another world, one that encompasses a dramatically different way of thinking about the press and about the role of public regulation in dealing with the concerns discussed in Chapter 2. It is as if the Court chose to experiment with a different way of ordering the world, something permitted, perhaps, by special circumstances (and I shall have more to say about that in the following two chapters), though such circumstances hardly justify the relish with which a fundamentally different approach was pursued. The Court seemed to enjoy the audacity of entertaining a conception of the world it had thoroughly rejected elsewhere.

Red Lion, therefore, reads like a tract that treats the press as the most serious threat to the ultimate First Amendment goal, the creation of an intelligent and informed democratic electorate. It is noteworthy that in its opinion the Court not once refers to the broadcast media as the "press," or to broadcasters as "journalists" or "editors." In the idiom chosen, broadcasters are referred to only as "licensees," "proxies," and "fiduciaries," or as the holders of "monopolies" capable of exercising "private censorship." Thus: "A license permits broadcasting, but the licensee has no constitutional right to be the one who holds the license or to monopolize a radio frequency to the exclusion of his fellow citizens. There is nothing in the First Amendment which prevents the Government from requiring a licensee to share his frequency with others and to conduct himself as a proxy or fiduciary with obligations to present those views and voices which are representative of his community and which would otherwise, by necessity, be barred from the airwaves."[34] Further: "It is the purpose of the First Amendment to preserve an uninhibited marketplace of ideas in which truth will ultimately prevail, rather than to countenance monopolization of that market, whether it be by the Government itself or a private licensee."[35]

In this universe, the medium is "collectively" owned, for free speech purposes, by the public: "But the people as a whole retain their interest in free speech by radio and their collective right to have the medium function consistently with the ends and purposes of the First Amendment."[36] Therefore, "[i]t is the right of the viewers and listeners, not the right of the broadcasters, which is paramount."[37]

Finally, in the triumvirate of parties that inhabit this universe, the public stands at the top and broadcasters at the bottom. The state, in the middle, executes the will of the people to insure that broadcasters provide adequate service to the realm of public debate: "It is the right of the public to receive suitable access to social, political, esthetic, moral, and other ideas and experiences which is crucial here. That right may not constitutionally be abridged either by Congress or by the FCC."[38]

In *Red Lion* the Court acted as if it were reviewing a decision of an ordinary administrative agency, to which great deference had to be paid to its expertise in dealing with a "new technology of communication." To the broadcasters' claim that right-of-reply regulations created an impermissible chilling effect, the Court deferred to the FCC's determination that the possibility of such an effect was "at best speculative."[39] To the broadcasters' claim that a shortage of frequencies no longer exists, due to technological innovations, the Court responded that it would not be influenced by the circumstances of the moment since this was a medium "for which wise planning is essential."[40]

III

It is difficult to appreciate both this extraordinary social experiment in public regulation of the mass media and what has been involved in these regulatory efforts to secure "equality" and "fairness" in public discussions. Three examples of fairness doctrine cases may serve to convey a flavor of the broadcast regulation project. In these three, the Federal Communications Commission and the federal Court of Appeals for the District of Columbia (the principal court of review for actions of the FCC) struggled to apply the doctrine. As I noted at the outset of this chapter, many regulations of the broadcast media have had as their purpose the protection of the quality of public discussion and decision making. But the fairness doctrine has been the most significant attempt yet to venture into the uncharted territory of using public institutions (administrative agencies and the courts) to help insure that the quality of public discussion in the mass media is at the desired level.

The Representative Patsy Mink case.[41] The first part of the fairness doctrine provides that broadcasters must devote a reasonable amount of airtime to the coverage of controversial issues of public importance. Whatever the market dictates, the fairness doctrine prohibits broadcasters from airing only entertainment programming; there also must be some presentation of information about public issues. In only one case, however, has the commission enforced this part of the fairness doctrine, and that case was *Patsy Mink.*

Representative Mink and others complained that West Virginia radio station WHAR had provided insufficient coverage of the political controversy over the continuation of strip mining in the region. That, the complainants said, was an important issue to the residents in the area served by WHAR. The station responded that it had received no requests for coverage from members of its audience, and that it had included in its newscasts some segments on the strip mining controversy provided by the Associated Press news service.

The commission found a violation. A station, it said, cannot rely on the absence of audience requests for programming on public issues. It has an affirmative obligation to provide coverage of important issues: "WHAR cannot rely on the fact that prior to this complaint it had not received any request for strip mining related programming, since it is the station's obligation to make an affirmative effort to program on issues of concern to its community."[42] The commission also evaluated the material the station had included in its programming and found it wanting. "It [the station] neither originated such programming nor provided syndicated material aimed at informing its listeners in any depth of the nature of the issue cited in the instant complaint—that issue being the effects of strip mining in and around Clarksburg."[43] The commission further expressed its dissatisfaction with the failure of the station management to maintain records of what material it had broadcast on public issues. "However, even more significant than the absence of locally originated programming on the issue of strip mining is the fact that WHAR cannot, with a reasonable degree of certainty, state what specific programming it has broadcast relating to this issue. '[W]e expect that licensees will be cognizant of the programming which has been presented on their stations, for it is difficult to see how a broadcaster who is ignorant of such matters could possibly be making a conscious and positive effort to meet his fairness obligations.'"[44]

The commission also received evidence on the question whether the issue of strip mining was of special importance to the community of Clarksburg. It is revealing to examine the commission's summary of the evidence it considered, including a reference to coverage by the local newspaper:

> In the present case the extensive amount of supporting material furnished by complainants sufficiently illustrates the fact that strip mining is of extreme importance to the people of Clarksburg. There is evidence from Congressional testimony, newspaper and magazine articles and research studies which illustrates the enormous impact strip mining has already had on the air and water quality and the immediate economic stability of the region. For example, Harrison County (Clarksburg and vicinity) has the highest percentage of strip mined land of any county in the State.

This information also reveals that the long term environmental picture and countless future employment opportunities in deep and surface mining and other related industries would be altered significantly by the mandatory reclamation of strip mined land provisions included in the legislation debated in Congress. The licensee has itself stated that strip mining is "a matter of importance to many of the inhabitants of the Clarksburg area." . . . Moreover, there is evidence of the highly controversial nature of the issue of strip mining, illustrated by citizen protests concerning strip mining in Clarksburg . . . , the nine "front page" stories in the *Clarksburg Telegram* over an eleven day period in July 1974, and the lengthy debate in Congress concerning the strip mining bill followed on May 20, 1975, by the President's veto of the measure. We believe it would be unreasonable for WHAR to deny that the issue of strip mining is a critical controversial issue of public importance in Clarksburg.[45]

The Cigarette Commercial Case (Banzhaf v. FCC).[46] In 1967, John F. Banzhaf, a law professor at George Washington University in Washington, D.C., filed a complaint with the commission charging that a CBS affiliate was violating the fairness doctrine by presenting only cigarette company commercials, specifically those "advertisements which by their portrayals of youthful or virile-looking or sophisticated persons enjoying cigarettes in interesting and exciting situations deliberately seek to create the impression and present the point of view that smoking is socially acceptable and desirable, manly, and a necessary part of a rich full life."[47] Banzhaf claimed that this constituted presentation of one side of a controversial issue of public importance and demanded free time for antismokers to present their views.

The commission ruled in Banzhaf's favor, saying that, in general, cigarette commercials advance the point of view, even if only implicitly, that smoking is desirable, which is itself a controversial issue of public importance. The commission was at pains to insist that the significance of the case was "limited to this product—cigarettes."[48] The case went on to the court of appeals, where it produced one of the most significant opinions on the fairness doctrine, written by a leading judge of the day, Chief Judge David Bazelon.

Bazelon refused to base his decision on the fairness doctrine exclusively, preferring instead to see the case as one arising under the general standard of the "public interest," which, he said, "indisputably includes the public health."[49] The court agreed with the commission that this was a "unique" situation, because cigarettes pose "a danger to life itself, . . . inherent in the normal use of the product, not one merely associated with its abuse or dependent on intervening fortuitous events," and because the product "threatens a substantial body of the population, not merely a peculiarly susceptible fringe group."[50] "Moreover," Bazelon wrote, "the danger, though not established beyond all doubt, is documented by a compelling cumulation of statistical evidence."[51]

The Court of Appeals agreed that the commission had properly evaluated the extent to which the public was receiving information about the dangers of smoking, but—and this is very important—in doing so the commission also had to consider not just the frequency or amount of information received but the public's capacity to understand and appreciate it. The commission could not rule out the possibility of irrationality:

> In these circumstances, the Commission could reasonably determine that news broadcasts, private and governmental educational programs, the information provided by other media, and the prescribed warnings on each cigarette pack, inadequately inform the public of the extent to which its life and health are most probably in jeopardy. The mere fact that information is available, or even that it is actually heard or read, does not mean that it is effectively understood. A man who hears a hundred "yeses" for each "no," when the actual odds lie heavily the other way, cannot be realistically deemed adequately informed. Moreover, since cigarette smoking is psychologically addicting, the confirmed smoker is likely to be relatively unreceptive to information about its dangers; his hearing is dulled by his appetite. And since it is so much harder to stop than not to

start, it is crucial that an accurate picture be communicated to those who have not yet begun.[52]

All this, the court said, spoke also to the First Amendment implications of the "cigarette ruling," but still more could be said on that score. The court showed some sympathy for the broadcaster's claim that the scarcity rationale was inadequate to support government regulation of the content of the broadcast media (*Banzhaf* was pre–*Red Lion*). But it found additional considerations supporting the regulatory structure.

In particular, the court referred to the "impact" of the broadcast media on the listener and viewer as a vital distinguishing characteristic justifying regulation:

> Written messages are not communicated unless they are read, and reading requires an affirmative act. Broadcast messages, in contrast, are "in the air." In an age of omnipresent radio, there scarcely breathes a citizen who does not know some part of a leading cigarette jingle by heart. Similarly, an ordinary habitual television watcher can *avoid* these commercials only by frequently leaving the room, changing the channel, or doing some other such affirmative act. It is difficult to calculate the subliminal impact of this pervasive propaganda, which may be heard even if not listened to, but it may reasonably be thought greater than the impact of the written word.[53]

In a footnote, the court continued:

> The effectiveness of the television commercial is hardly disputed, for it alone appeals to both of man's most receptive senses—hearing and seeing. . . . Psychological memory experiments indicate strongly that people tend to remember advertising messages presented by a combination of visual and auditory methods significantly more than those presented by either method alone.[54]

As for the specific cigarette ruling, the court found it acceptable under the First Amendment, observing that it did not censor or prohibit speech, that cigarette advertisers and stations were unlikely to be chilled by the ruling (and, even if they were, this kind of speech is of low First Amendment value), and that any such costs would be outweighed by the increase in information the ruling would make available to the public.

The Pensions case (National Broadcasting Co. v. FCC).[55] In 1972, NBC broadcast a documentary entitled "Pensions: The Broken Promise." The program recounted the life stories of several individuals who claimed they had been unfairly deprived of their pensions. NBC received several awards for this documentary, including the George Foster Peabody Award and an Emmy nomination. It was also sued. Accuracy in Media (AIM), a public interest organization, filed a complaint with the FCC charging that NBC had presented only one side of a controversial issue of public importance, namely, the need for comprehensive reform of the private pension system in the United States. The commission agreed with AIM and ordered NBC to provide reasonable coverage of the other side. NBC took the case to the federal court of appeals.

Again, a distinguished federal judge, Harold Leventhal, wrote a major opinion that struggled with the issue of how to define "fairness" in the discussion of important public issues. He wrote the majority opinion for the panel of three; one judge dissented. The outcome was a ruling in favor of NBC, overturning the decision of the commission.

The case is analytically complex but interesting because of that. AIM argued that the pensions documentary primarily supported those who were arguing at the time that Congress should enact—as it eventually did—comprehensive legislation overhauling the private pension system. NBC responded with a subtle, even clever, argument. It is true, the network said, that a small part of the program involved comments on the need for overall reform; indeed, the last words on the program were those of the narrator Edwin Newman:

These are matters for Congress to consider and, indeed, the Senate Labor Committee is considering them now. They are also matters for those who are in pension plans. If you're in one, you might find it useful to take a close look at it. Our own conclusion about all of this, is that it is almost inconceivable that this enormous thing has been allowed to grow up with so little understanding of it and with so little protection and such uneven results for those involved. The situation, as we've seen it, is deplorable.[56]

Despite this, said NBC, the show was internally balanced on the issue, with commentary against reform included as well. The bulk of the show, it argued, simply presented a series of individuals describing their perceived mistreatment under particular pension programs. NBC claimed that all this amounted to, for fairness doctrine purposes, an assertion that *some* pension programs were flawed—a proposition no one in the political arena disputed. Similarly, the assertion that some legislation was required was not in itself a "controversial issue" since nearly everyone accepted the need for some kind of regulation.

Levanthal accepted NBC's argument that the documentary was primarily a program about *some* abuses in *some* programs. To the extent that it engaged the larger, and very controversial, issue of overall reform, the program was found to be sufficiently balanced. Levanthal entered into a lengthy discussion of the importance of this kind of "investigative reporting" for the provision of public information, and the importance of not discouraging such reporting by too rigorously demanding fairness. Unfortunately, along the way in this discussion some rather silly things were said about the fairness doctrine. It was stated, for example, that the fairness doctrine demands balance within a specific program, which it does not; that it requires "equivalent" exposure of other viewpoints, which it also does not; and that the crucial issue is whether an exposé must present examples of good apples along with its presentation of rotten ones, when in fact the fairness doctrine claim is that there must be a fuller discussion of the *significance* and extent of the rottenness for purposes of thinking about public policy. Like all of us, Levanthal was writing for, and in, his moment, and at that time investigative journalism was highly respected, even glamorous, and the idea was growing that broadcasters are journalists—themes I will turn to in Chapter 5.

While these are interesting issues, I wish to emphasize a different aspect of the case. For our purposes, the outcome is less important than seeing how these issues were addressed in the fora of a public agency and a court, not just in editorial offices. Two facts about the case then become significant. First, it is noteworthy that the court engaged in a lengthy, in-depth review of the documentary. A complete transcript of the program was attached as an appendix to the opinion. In order to decide whether the "dominant thrust" of the program concerned the overall performance of the pension system, or only certain abuses in some programs, and to determine whether the discussion of overall performance was in fact balanced, Leventhal's opinion reviews the contemporaneous commentary of twenty-five television columnists, then parses the program in depth, listing seriatim "adverse comments on overall performance" and then "favorable comments on overall performance."[57] This was, by any standard, a close reading of the documentary text.

Second, the *Pensions* case was significant because it clearly revealed, like its predecessor *Banzhaf,* how any effort to understand the nature of fair political discussion necessarily entails understanding how people think and the impact of a medium on their thinking. As Kalven said of *New York Times v. Sullivan,* the Court must in the end—if it is to be a sophisticated analyst—develop a psychology of people. In *Pensions,* the debate between the majority and the dissent was really, and most significantly, about how one should assume people interpret a program about a series of abuses or the costs of a given social policy. Do viewers become outraged at identified injustices and jump to the conclusion that something should be done about it, forgetting or never realizing that all systems are imperfect and that sometimes the costs of improvements outweigh the costs of the original imperfections? (It is interesting that here the press denied the presence of psychological bias, but recall from the third chapter how the press knows this phenomenon well when it comes to its own First Amendment claims and relies on the courts to protect it against this precise impulse.) Or do they watch such an exposé critically and wait for further information before reaching a final judgment?

The point is that the fairness doctrine eventually brings one to a general exploration of the biases in public thinking, just as the interest in fairness and justice in the trial process brings one to do the same in fashioning the rules of evidence for our system of criminal and civil trials—an analogy I shall return to at the end of this book.

IV

The foregoing provides a glimpse into the remarkable experience of government regulation of a branch of the press, intervention designed to improve the quality of public discussion. Our object has not been to evaluate how well this was done, nor, assuming it was done about as well as could be expected, whether it has been worth it. How to go about making such an evaluation—something society must confront in the near future—will be taken up below. Surely, however, it should be apparent by now that this is an area of the law worthy of attention and study. Yet it is an odd fact of life—one whose significance we will begin to assess in the next chapter—that even most First Amendment experts know very little about it. Neither *Patsy Mink,* nor *Banzhaf,* nor the *Pensions* case are to be found in any major constitutional law text, though they loom large in the jurisprudence of the fairness doctrine.

Before closing this chapter I should add a few comments on the course of history of the fairness doctrine and the cases discussed above. *Banzhaf,* as already noted, was a major case in the area of public regulation of media in part because it was the first to wrestle with the difficult question of how to address the psychological impact of the various media, and in part because it was the first to extend the doctrine (or the umbrella "public interest" concept) to the implicit messages of commercials. Though both the commission and the court of appeals were careful to try to limit the reach of the decision, claiming that, as "a cigarette case," it involved a very special product (one that poses "a danger to life itself"), case after case involving commercial messages continued to come before the commission.

This occurred during the activist era of civil rights, Vietnam, and the beginnings of the environmental movement. The fairness doctrine, along with such other public regulations as the proxy solicitation rule, was seized upon by political groups as a means of making their views known. Implicit messages were found in every commercial, many addressing controversial issues of public importance, and many products came to be seen as posing a threat to life: advertisements for the armed forces (held not within *Banzhaf*),[58] and for high-powered automobiles (the commission held not within *Banzhaf* but the court of appeals reversed).[59] In 1974 the commission issued a report in which it reversed the course it had embarked upon with *Banzhaf*. It stated that in the future it would not apply the fairness doctrine to commercials unless the advertisement made a "meaningful statement which obviously addresses, and advocates a point of view on, a controversial issue of public importance."[60] While a year later an environmental group took the occasion of a fairness doctrine complaint against commercials for snowmobiles to claim that the new policy was inconsistent with the commission's statutory obligations, the court of appeals upheld the commission's choice of self-restraint in the area of commercials, and the policy has remained in effect ever since.[61] Cigarette commercials were not affected by the 1974 policy shift, because Congress had acted, shortly after *Banzhaf*, to ban such commercials from the airwaves after 1971.[62] Cigarette companies sued, claiming that antismoking commercials, which were still prevalent, presented one side of a controversial issue of public importance and asking for the opportunity to respond. The claim was rejected on the ground that the congressional decision to ban cigarettes as a health hazard definitively resolved the issue and made it no longer "controversial."[63]

The *Pensions* case also has a tangled history. After the thorough and contested decision by the panel of the court of appeals, an *en banc* hearing of the entire court was called, which itself produced many opinions by various judges (including Leventhal). But before a decision of the full court was reached Congress enacted comprehensive pension reform legislation. The court then decided that the fairness issue was moot and dismissed the case, an action that itself produced an array of opinions.[64]

In recent years the fairness doctrine has been beleaguered. Under the Reagan administration's general policy of deregulation, the commission has done all it can to limit, and even abolish, the doctrine (although, ironically, it found a fairness violation in one major case, involving commercials by a utility company in favor of a proposed nuclear power plant).[65] In a 1985 report, issued after lengthy public hearings, the commission advocated that the fairness doctrine be abandoned.[66] Today there is a stalemate on the question. The commission has taken a general position against continued enforcement, while Congress, which in general seems to favor the doctrine, is considering legislation specifically incorporating it into the Communications Act.[67]

Taken together, this chapter paints a picture of a massive regulatory enterprise aimed at insuring fairness in the media of television and radio. Most important, perhaps, it also conveys some notion of how the operations of the doctrine have drawn those involved into a difficult study, not only of what constitutes "fairness" in the presentation of information but of questions about how information is received and its impact on the audience. By its very nature, the doctrine forces us to think about problems of bias and irrationality in our own thought processes. Such self-reflection is surely a good thing, but whether public institutions should be exploring it through the procedures of law is another question. We have seen that one by-product of the First Amendment is the opportunities it provides for self-definition and self-reflection. Judges and others who set about trying to solve particular problems need theories about the world in order to do so. The fairness doctrine, which is really a very young idea, has provided the initial means for an exploration of bias and irrationality in public thinking about public issues.

The Power of the
Potential Analogy

O nce one appreciates the history of extensive public regulation, throughout this century, of the electronic media,
the problem arises of how to *interpret* the relationship between
that system and the principle of autonomy as applied to the print
media.

The primary thesis I want to consider is that the broadcast
experience has not been simply a marginal enterprise but one
that has exerted a profound influence over the judicial approach
toward, and the behavior of, the "autonomous" print media.
The same point can be put another way. Despite popular attitudes to the contrary, this country has never had a modern press
largely free of government controls over the content of what is
published. Rather, we have had a dual system in which only one
branch of the press is autonomous. The other branch, the electronic media, has undergone continuing experimentation with
public regulation, always with the potential for spreading
throughout the media as a whole. The print media, therefore,
has lived under the threat that broadcasting will suddenly become a relevant, living analogy for the future of the press generally. And, through the process of implementing public regulations of the electronic media, the print media has also lived in
a world in which government and the courts continuously issue
normative statements (in the context of deciding actual cases)
about what constitutes good journalism.

In other words, in my judgment—and this is clearly one of
those matters on which facts are elusive and a judgment is all one
can reasonably pretend to have—broadcast regulation has not
been an isolated, aberrant, self-contained experience but one
with a spreading influence. And, if that is true, then freedom of

the press in this country has never meant, and does not mean today, the absence of government control.

For many reasons it is important to know whether this is true. In particular, we face the practical problem of deciding what to do in the future. Currently our dual system of the press is undergoing increasing scrutiny and reevaluation. Many people—administrators, legislators, judges, and academics—are focusing on the question whether this system ought to be made unitary. Should we move to a single system with an autonomous press, following exclusively the model of the print media? Should we have an entirely regulated press, along the lines of the model of the electronic media? Should we continue with the dual system? Or should we embrace any one of the innumerable variations on these possibilities? The weight of opinion at the moment seems to have shifted toward adopting a unitary print media model for the entire mass media, but it is too early to tell whether that view will prevail.

In designing institutional arrangements for the future, we often look to past experience for guidance. But to do so we must address two major issues. First, we must come to some understanding of that experience: how it worked, what was good about it, what was bad, and whether it was consistent with principles of sound public policy and constitutional law. Second, we must determine the relevance of that past experience to the future we imagine. A mistake of the past *may* be a mistake for the future. It is, however, not always so. Circumstances may be different today. What was once wrong may now be right. Indeed, it is always possible, in the continuous irony of life, that a mistaken policy of the past may have caused or contributed to a change in circumstances, the sow's ear, as it were, turning itself into the silk purse. And so one must ascertain to what extent the world of the present and future differs from the world of the past.

It should also be emphasized that part of the reevaluation process involves constitutional law: whether the ever-changing tradition of the First Amendment will or should impose limitations on the types of arrangements we might consider. For reasons I take up in the next chapter, this also should lead us to want to interpret and assess past experience.

Finally, other questions should be asked in addition to those designed to elicit information about the impact of the broadcast regulatory system on the print media. Specifically, we should ask the converse question, namely, What has been the impact of the principle of autonomy, as developed in the print media, on the regulatory system for broadcasting? And we should further ask what the overall experience of the last half-century can teach us about how this society treats new technologies of communication.

I

As I have indicated, many contemporary observers argue that the regulatory system covering broadcasting must be discarded and those media fully incorporated into the First Amendment principles that have been fashioned to govern print.[1] A few advocate a reverse arrangement.[2] That is not a debate I wish to enter right now. Rather I want to grapple with the preliminary question whether, and to what extent, we can regard the experience of the past sixty years as relevant to the debate about what to do in the future. For example, can we assume that, since the print media system has worked fairly well, it will continue to do so in a future in which the electronic media operates under the same principles?

In thinking about these questions it is important to begin by identifying two highly significant and generally unchallengeable facts about the broadcast regulation experience. These may be added to observations made in the preceding chapter about how the Supreme Court has assumed broadcasting to be *different* from the print media—and therefore subject to public regulation—and how it has actually celebrated such regulation. All these observations must eventually be examined to determine whether they can yield a coherent understanding of the complex system of freedom of the press as it has existed in this country during this century.

[A]

It is a decisive fact about broadcast regulation that the primary rationales used to justify that system, which involved attempts to distinguish broadcast from print media, are illogical. In this discussion, it should be kept in mind that the same rationales have been used to justify broadcast regulation both as public policy and under the First Amendment.

Recall Justice Frankfurter's argument in the 1943 *NBC* decision that broadcasting is "unique" among methods of expression: "Freedom of utterance is abridged to many who wish to use the limited facilities of radio. Unlike other modes of expression, radio inherently is not available to all. That is its unique characteristic, and that is why, unlike other modes of expression, it is subject to governmental regulation."[3] This "scarcity rationale" focused on the finite nature of the electromagnetic spectrum, which permits fewer parties to use it effectively than may desire to speak. This supposedly distinguishing feature has been repeated endlessly in commission and judicial decisions over the years as the central justification for government regulation of broadcasting.

Recall also how *Red Lion* gave this rationale its modern articulation. The Court began its analysis of the broadcaster's First Amendment objection to the fairness doctrine (and related rules) by observing how "differences in the characteristics of new media justify differences in the First Amendment standards applied to them."[4] These differences centered on the fact that "only a tiny fraction of those with resources and intelligence can hope to communicate by radio at the same time if intelligible communication is to be had, even if the entire radio spectrum is utilized in the present state of commercially acceptable technology."[5] Without regulation there would be "chaos," and "[w]here there are substantially more individuals who want to broadcast than there are frequencies to allocate, it is idle to posit an unabridgeable First Amendment right to broadcast comparable to the right of every individual to speak, write, or publish."[6]

The premise of *Red Lion* seemed to be that our society faced a choice between the risks of government regulation and an effective broadcast media and an unregulated but ineffective media beset with the mutual interference of broadcasting multitudes. This was, in reality, a Hobson's Choice, the only sensible answer being that the government had to intervene to allocate the spectrum. But the fortunate few who obtained the precious licenses could reasonably be expected to share with those less fortunate. "A license permits broadcasting, but the licensee has no constitutional right to be the one who holds the license or to monopolize a radio frequency to the exclusion of his fellow citizens. There is nothing in the First Amendment which prevents the Government from requiring a licensee to share his frequency with others and to conduct himself as a proxy or fiduciary with obligations to present those views and voices which are representative of his community and which would otherwise, by necessity, be barred from the airwaves."[7]

Thus, "[b]ecause of the scarcity of radio frequencies, the Government is permitted to put restraints on licensees in favor of others whose views should be expressed on this unique medium."[8] While broadcasters surely have First Amendment interests deserving of protection, it is "the right of the viewers and listeners, not the right of the broadcasters, which is paramount."[9]

Now, there is a devastating—even embarrassing—deficiency in this analysis. These facts that more people would like to broadcast than there is space to accommodate them in the electromagnetic spectrum, and that without some system of allocation the phenomenon of interference will make the medium useless, may be true, but it does not follow that the only possible method of allocation is through government licensing and regulation. There are alternatives, the most important being the system of private property rights and a market. Developing a system of property rights in the spectrum, just as has been done with land, would permit the sale, or gift, of spectrum space, which would in turn allow the marketplace to discipline broadcasters into meeting the "public interest."

If a market system, with private property rights, could work to avoid "chaos" within the broadcast media and meet the public interest, then the question should be whether there is any reason why—in public policy or First Amendment terms—we ought to prefer a free market system over a government licensing-with-regulation system. Based on the discussion in the preceding chapter, one serious consideration comes immediately to mind. From *Sullivan,* with its striking central image of the regime of seditious libel, we know that the First Amendment embodies a concern over regulation of the press because of the government's tendency to exceed its authority and censor what should be left alone. While this may not be the decisive consideration on the issue of the legitimacy of broadcast regulation, it certainly cannot be ignored. It is, in fact, a central issue, but it is avoided by the simple-minded and erroneous assertion that public regulation is the only allocation scheme that can avoid chaos in broadcasting.

Although the scarcity, or "remedy for chaos," rationale has been the official rationale for broadcast regulation, another rationale is sometimes offered. It, too, is presented on the assumption that regulation can be justified only by locating a material difference between broadcast and print media. The argument is that, since broadcasting makes use of a "public resource," namely, the electromagnetic spectrum (which Congress in the original statutes declared to be public property), and since broadcasters use it only with the permission of the public, it is entirely appropriate for the public to impose conditions on its use.[10] But, as with the scarcity thesis, the public property rationale fails as a distinction, for the simple reason that the print media also makes use of public property—the streets and sidewalks upon which newspapers and magazines are delivered.

[B]

The second important feature about the system of broadcast regulation is that, for most of its life, it seems to have been either ignored or, when seen, accorded the unqualified endorsement of the First Amendment community. In many respects, the broadcast experience *seems* to have been an isolated one.

In an article in 1976,[11] I wrote the following (and I believe still accurate) description of how the system has been received: The phenomenon of broadcast regulation has, in many respects, the qualities of an historical accident. An examination of its origins and development reveals the striking ease with which it slid into our political and constitutional system. One stark fact is apparent: society obviously has thought differently about broadcasting than it has about the print media. Certainly doubts and objections have been raised periodically, but on the whole there have not been the outcries against censorship that would undoubtedly have occurred if regulation had been imposed on newspapers. "In brief," Harry Kalven said in 1967, "we all take as commonplace a degree of government surveillance for broadcasting which would by instant reflex ignite the fiercest protest were it found in other areas of communication."[12]

Broadcasters, although often lamenting what they considered to be public insensitivity to their First Amendment rights, have also been conspicuously unassertive of those rights. Kalven noted how "the [broadcasting] industry has under-estimated its legal position and given up too soon."[13] Major First Amendment theorists—among them Zechariah Chafee,[14] the Hutchins Commission on Freedom of the Press,[15] Alexander Meiklejohn,[16] William O. Douglas,[17] Hugo Black,[18] and Thomas Emerson[19]— have all stated at one time or another that regulation of broadcasting is obviously appropriate. Even the scholarly community has tended to overlook the significance of the constitutional treatment of broadcasting. Major casebooks published as late as 1965,[20] for example, did not even mention either the existence of broadcast regulation or the seminal *NBC* decision. Even after *Red Lion,* casebooks did not present broadcast regulations as posing a significant constitutional dilemma; broadcast decisions were merely described briefly in a note format.[21] A major constitutional law casebook, published in 1975, relegated broadcast decisions to a textual note (instead of reproducing the cases, as is done with major decisions), failed to address the broader First Amendment significance of the decision to regulate, and provided no cross-reference to *Miami Herald,* which was included in the materials covering libel. If the scholars who formulate and organize for study the most pressing issues under the First Amendment fail to find any particular significance in broadcast regulation, other than as a minor exception to the general rules, it is not surprising that society, too, has failed to recognize broadcast cases as a major departure from traditional First Amendment principles.

Part of this isolation of the broadcast experience occurred through the language used to discuss it. It will be recalled that the Supreme Court in *Red Lion* never referred to the broadcast media as the press nor to broadcasters as editors or journalists; they were consistently described as licensees and fiduciaries.

91

In the early years, especially, but even as late as 1973 (the year in which *Columbia Broadcasting System v. Democratic National Committee* was decided and the first time the Supreme Court referred to broadcasters as journalists and editors), only occasionally was this practice of linguistic isolation broken. The Hutchins commission, it is true, used the term "press" inclusively: "At its first meeting the Commission decided to include within its scope the major agencies of mass communication: the radio, newspapers, motion pictures, magazines, and books. Wherever the word 'press' is used in the publications of the Commission, it refers to all these media."[22] It is also worth noting that one of the commission's recommendations was that "the constitutional guarantees of the freedom of the press be recognized as including the radio and motion pictures."[23] What this meant to the commission, however, and what it has meant to many other First Amendment advocates, was something far different from the constitutional guarantees accorded to the print media:

> In the case of radio this recommendation would give constitutional support to the prohibition against censorship in the Communications Act. It would not prevent the Federal Communications Commission from denying a license on the ground that the applicant was unprepared to serve the public interest, convenience, and necessity. Nor would it prevent the Commission from considering, in connection with an application for renewal, whether the applicant had kept the promises he made when the license was granted and had actually served the public interest, convenience, and necessity. This recommendation is intended to strengthen the prohibition against censorship, not to guarantee licensees a perpetual franchise regardless of their performance. The air belongs to the public, not to the radio industry.[24]

II

It would be reasonable to conclude from the foregoing observations that the broadcast regulatory experiment has been so isolated in the minds of observers that it has had little impact beyond its own limited borders. That the major rationales behind it are weak and illogical does nothing to discredit the fact that people may have fervently believed in their validity, which for purposes of assessing the broader relevance of the regulatory system is all that really matters. If everyone assumes that broadcasting is different, and different in a way that makes it unique for First Amendment purposes, then we would seem to have no reason to think that the print media should fear its potential relevance. The apparent fact that virtually everyone ignores it, or talks about it in language that isolates it from print, only reinforces that view.

While there is a good deal of truth in this conclusion, it is not the full truth. The relationship between the electronic media and its treatment and the print media and its treatment is subtle, shifting, and reciprocal. This may be seen more clearly from another perspective, one I would describe as the shaping influence of the potential analogy.

While the scarcity rationale (and the public resource, or ownership, rationale) was flawed but believed, its unmasking was not recent. It began with an article in the mid-1960s by a well-known economist, Ronald Coase,[25] who pointed out the universality of the condition of scarcity. Although he recommended that broadcasting be accorded the same constitutional freedoms as print,[26] rejection of the technical scarcity claim does not logically foreclose the possibility of other rationales for differential treatment of broadcasting.

The problem was, and still is, that the scarcity rationale is ambiguous as it is typically expressed. As a claim that broadcasting is unique because it makes use of a finite resource, or because without some method of allocation it would be effectively unusable, it is incorrect. But as a statement that the resource broadcasting needs in order to communicate is too limited, too finite in amount, so that too few people—that is, too few for First Amendment purposes—are able to communicate by that medium—and that, therefore, the normal assumptions underlying the First Amendment commitment to press freedom from government regulation do not apply to that medium, and some allowance for government intervention must be granted—

is not an irrational or illogical assertion at all. It is a perfectly sensible thing to say. The only difficulty lies in the implication of this *for the print media*. The question is whether the print media—and especially daily newspapers—are not equally, or even more, restricted in numbers of outlets than broadcast stations. If that is so, then this new rationale for broadcast regulation might apply equally to the regulation of newspapers.

This produces another argument. Are newspapers in fact more restricted than broadcast stations? A typical community has one daily newspaper and several radio and television stations. There are roughly 1,700 daily newspapers in the country and 13,000 broadcast stations. On the other hand, there are only approximately 550 VHF commercial television stations, and the bulk of the programming on these stations is controlled by three networks. But it is also true that an oligopoly of wire services and chain ownership dictate nearly all the national news reported in daily papers. The argument continues. At some point, one begins to realize that the problem of comparison can become even more complex as the classes being compared are redefined. Why should the comparison be between broadcast stations (or even television stations) and daily newspapers? Why not compare broadcasting and all forms of print media, including books, magazines, shoppers, and pamphlets.[27] Rarely is it realized that the real question is not whether the print media (however defined) are more numerous, or less restricted, than broadcasting but whether they, too, exceed the allowable level of concentration for purposes of deserving autonomy status under the First Amendment.

The argument over the potential similarity of broadcast and print has yet another branch. Assuming that print does exceed some "allowable" limit of concentration, does it make a difference, in terms of First Amendment analysis, how that concentration evolved? Broadcasting is concentrated because the electromagnetic spectrum can physically handle only so many users. But clearly enough paper and steel are available to allow us more daily newspapers. Economic factors are most commonly cited to explain the enormous reduction in the number of daily newspapers during this century. The phenomenon of economies of scale makes it possible for larger enterprises to produce each paper more cheaply. But, granting such differences in the cause of concentration in each media, the key question is why (for First Amendment purposes) these differences should matter at all. The central point of tracing this difficult, intricate argument is not to judge which position is right but to show how it is *reasonably arguable* that broadcast regulation may well be the relevant analogy for print. Recognition of the ambiguity residing in the meaning of the scarcity rationale, and the possibility that it points to a phenomenon common to the media as a whole rather than to something peculiar to broadcasting, was, furthermore, in the air at least by the 1960s. In 1967, Professor Jerome Barron (later dean of George Washington University Law School) wrote a widely read law review article in which he argued forcefully that newspapers had reached such a level of concentration, of dominance over the marketplace of ideas in local communities, that they should be regarded for First Amendment purposes as public utilities or common carriers, along the lines of the broadcast media.[28] They should, for example, be subject to a rule of nondiscrimination in selling advertising space. It cannot, therefore, reasonably be claimed, at least by the 1960s, that the idea of transferring broadcast-style regulations to the print media was unthinkable.

That brings us back to *Red Lion* in 1969. In the preceding chapter, I suggested that the extraordinary, really distinguishing, characteristic of that opinion was that it embraced public regulation of broadcasting with such enthusiasm. The Court offered its wholehearted endorsement, going well beyond what was called for even if one believes (as the Court professed to) that the scarcity rationale identifies a valid distinction between print and broadcasting. Recall that the Court's opinion in *Red Lion* never mentioned the print media, nor the traditional concern about government abuse of its power over the press. The central image was not the regime of "seditious libel" but the regime of "private censorship." This posture may have constituted a commitment to keeping a complete separation, a Chinese wall, between broadcasting and print.

But there is another possible interpretation. *Red Lion* may be seen as an experiment in rethinking the relationship between the government, the public, and the press in modern society. In a sense, public regulation was being tried on for size. It was as if no other world, no world of an autonomous press, existed. And if this was true, then there was good reason for the print media to become alarmed. Shortly afterward, in fact, Professor Barron wrote of how the *Red Lion* decision was a *media,* not a broadcast, decision. To Barron the Court was moving toward adoption of the position he had taken in 1967.[29] In the end, of course, the Court did not. In 1974, it decided *Miami Herald v. Tornillo* and held that the public access concept had no citizenship in the realm of newspapers. It did so emphatically, and without any reference to *Red Lion* or to broadcast regulation. And, significantly, Jerome Barron was the losing counsel.

It has been a mark of the Court's performance in this area of the First Amendment to be ambiguous—to be self-blinding but also to be coy. After *Miami Herald*, the *Red Lion* decision was cast in doubt, a situation that endured until *Columbia Broadcasting System v. FCC*[30] was decided seven years later. In that decision the Court upheld the reasonable access rule and, in so doing, gave no hint that it intended broadcast regulation to be affected by *Miami Herald*. Until *Miami Herald*, however, it was unclear what the scope of *Red Lion* would be.

This ambiguity about the status of broadcast regulation, and its potential relevance for the rest of the media, may well have influenced developments in print journalism. At the very least, it contributed to making the interpretation of public regulations in the broadcast media, and especially the fairness doctrine, relevant statements about the proper standards of journalism for the media generally.[31] Whatever their ultimate legitimacy as regulations, there can be little doubt that they have constituted an expression of values, having obvious relevance wherever media power exists. Here again, as with the phenomenon of Supreme Court decisions affecting the character of the press, we have similar difficulties in analyzing, or even proving, such an influence. Still, if only intuitively, it seems plausible that the idea of fairness and balance in journalism was reinforced by its very real—and looming—regulatory presence in the broadcast media context.[32] It seems more than coincidental, for example, that the now widespread institution of the "op. ed." page in newspapers was first instituted by the *New York Times* in the year following the Supreme Court's decision in *Red Lion*.[33]

III

We should also consider the possibility that, if it is reasonable to think that the existence of the system of broadcast regulation influenced other media, it may be equally reasonable (though admittedly not logically compelled) to think that there has been an influence in the other direction—from print to broadcast—as well. A reciprocal relationship of influence between the legal concepts in the print and broadcast media seems plausible. Such a relationship, however, might be of two kinds.

The first would be the reverse of the phenomenon we have just considered of the restraining influence on print of the potential extension of the broadcast regulatory model. In other words, we must consider the possibility that the system of broadcast regulation has worked as well as it has (and the general view has been that it has been afflicted rarely by government excesses)[34] primarily because it evolved in a context in which the dominant principle was that of an autonomous press.

There is a second and altogether different interpretation of the dual system we have had. The purpose of regulation may be viewed, not as a partial remedy to a problem common to all media, with the autonomous press serving as a restraining influence on potentially overeager regulators of broadcasting, but as a vehicle for instilling journalistic values in a new and as yet ethically unformed medium. One might think of this as, in essence, a school of journalism for new media that uses the espoused ethics of the print media as its model. Indeed, it is difficult to examine the experience of broadcast regulation in this country, to follow it closely, and not to sense that regulation was imposed early and comprehensively, and upheld by the Court later and casually, because it is recognized that freedom of the press (as the Hutchins commission argued) depends upon certain minimal conditions of journalistic capability being achieved and because there is considerable uncertainty about whether new media will satisfy those conditions. This may explain why so many people are uncharacteristically, inexplicably receptive to the many types of government regulation undertaken in relation to the electronic media.

Why do new media produce this kind of reaction? Several factors may be involved.

One is that new media are unknown and untested. They are perceived as having enormous potential, which might be lost unless regulated, and enormous danger, which might cause harm unless regulated. Comments of both kinds abound throughout the judicial opinions in the broadcast area. Broadcasting is always said to be "dynamic" and in "flux."

Another significant factor is that new media tend to be owned and staffed by people whose experience is in business and entertainment. This has two important consequences. First, although the Court held in 1948 (in *U.S. v. Paramount Pictures, Inc.*)[35] that the First Amendment protects entertainment speech as well as political speech, it seems likely that the small amount of news content in broadcasting as a whole made government regulation all the more acceptable (and arguably necessary).[36] Second, new media owners, as business people, are unaccustomed and generally ill-disposed toward asserting First Amendment rights. Moreover, journalists in the traditional media are reluctant to assist those in the new media in asserting their rights. There is a startling and revealing fact on this point: print media organizations have never filed briefs in support of the broadcaster's claims for First Amendment rights. Ask any print journalist what he or she thinks of broadcast journalists, and, at least until very recently, the likely answer would be that the term is an oxymoron.

Finally, sometimes when new media arise, as was the case with broadcasting, the government must intervene to bring order to the system. Once the process has begun, further government intrusion may seem more palatable.

Whatever the causes, it is instructive to retrace the remarkable progression from the *NBC* case in 1943, where broadcast regulation was casually upheld; to *Red Lion* in 1969, in which a full-scale opinion justified and extolled the system of regulation; to the 1973 decision of *CBS v. Democratic National Committee,* where the Court rejected the claim for a public right to purchase airtime to discuss public issues, and in so doing referred to broadcasters—for the first time—as "editors" and "journalists"; and on to recent times as the movement for integration of broadcasting within the print model has achieved full momentum. It is a progression that seems scripted to coincide with the growth of the new medium as a true journalistic enterprise.

IV

To support these general observations about how new technologies of communication are only gradually absorbed into the traditions of the First Amendment, it is helpful to consider the stunningly parallel history of Supreme Court cases involving regulation of cable television. In many ways the gradual absorption of cable into First Amendment analysis is similar to what happened with respect to the broadcast media. One cannot understand the development of the idea of freedom of the press without taking into account this remarkable history of cable regulation.

Cable television was introduced in the United States in the late 1940s. In the beginning it primarily served rural areas where television antennae were outside the signal range of broadcasters. This function continued throughout much of the 1950s. Toward the end of that decade the service began to change. Cable companies entered markets already served by existing broadcast stations and imported the signals of more distant, and otherwise unavailable, broadcast stations. This encroachment into existing markets led to a movement within the broadcast industry to bring cable under FCC authority and regulation. The FCC declined.[37] The Communications Act, it reasoned, applied only to "common carriers" (telephone and telegraph services) or to "broadcasters," and cable fit into neither category. It was up to Congress, the commission said, to decide whether to amend the act to encompass the new technology. Congress, however, did nothing.

In the 1960s the FCC gradually began to reverse its earlier decision not to take jurisdiction of cable. The entering wedge was microwave facilities, which many cable companies used to relay signals. Because these facilities boosted broadcast signals, the FCC concluded that such operations constituted "broadcasting" and so claimed a peg on which to assert jurisdiction.[38] Within a few years the FCC required cable systems served by microwave to carry the signals of any station in the community in which they operated (the "must-carry" rule).[39] It also forbade such systems from duplicating the programming of local stations for a specific period of time before and after local broadcast (the "nonduplication" rule).[40] In 1966, the commission removed the microwave qualification and applied both rules to virtually all cable systems. In a dramatic move, it also instituted a freeze on the growth of the new technology by restricting cable systems in the top 100 markets from further importation of distant signals unless the commission explicitly granted an exception.[41]

This last development brought the issue of the legitimacy of cable regulation before the Supreme Court in 1968. In *United States v. Southwestern Cable Co.,*[42] a television broadcaster in San Diego had petitioned the commission for a decision barring a local cable system, Southwestern Cable from importing broadcast signals from Los Angeles into the San Diego market. The commission proceeded with the case and temporarily constrained the cable system from importing any new signals. Southwestern went to court to challenge the commission's jurisdictional authority.

The Supreme Court unanimously upheld the authority of the commission to regulate cable under the Communications Act. As in the 1943 decision on broadcast regulation (*National Broadcasting Co. v. United States*), the tone of the *Southwestern Cable* opinion emphasized the need to afford government great leeway in dealing with the problems raised by a new, "dynamic" medium.[43] In the Court's view the language of the Communications Act, the provisions of which apply to "all interstate and foreign communication by wire or radio," was sufficient to encompass the technology of cable since it involves "communication by wire."[44] Although Congress had no notion of cable technology when it enacted the Communications Act, it did want to afford the commission "a comprehensive mandate," one with "not niggardly but expansive powers" (quoting from the decision in *NBC*).[45] With regard to the particular set of regulations challenged in this case, the Court held that the commission had carefully and reasonably determined that they were necessary to deflect the threat posed by the new cable technology to the commission's longstanding effort to encourage the development of local broadcasters, which the commission had tried (without great success, however) to implement through its original allocation of broadcast licenses and through the encouragement of ultrahigh frequency (UHF) and educational stations.[46] Therefore, the Court concluded, the commission had the power to issue all regulations "reasonably ancillary to the effective performance of the Commission's various responsibilities for the regulation of television broadcasting."[47]

Here, then, was another extraordinary Supreme Court decision bearing on the fundamental question of the scope of government involvement in the development of new media. To understand just how remarkable it was, we must consider it in a larger context, and, as with the broadcasting cases, be prepared to take note of what was not stated as much as of what was said. Perhaps the most striking feature of the Court's opinion was the absence of any acknowledgment by the justices of the potential argument that cable technology could undermine a principal rationale for regulation of the broadcast media, one the Court itself had proferred in *NBC* and in *Red Lion*. That is, if the constitutional justification for permitting government oversight of the electronic media is the relative "physical scarcity" of frequencies available for use, then cable technology—with its capacity for introducing a very large number of channels—promises an end to it.[48] One would expect that a court as leery of government involvement with the press as the Supreme Court professed to be in cases involving print would have seized upon this apparent potential of cable technology to eliminate the need for government regulation of the electronic media. Instead of encouraging regulation that would stifle its growth, the Court might have denied regulatory authority altogether or permitted it only on the condition that it be designed to maximize the technology's potential. But the Court took a different path, one in which public regulation was encouraged. The Communications Act was interpreted expansively, not restrictively, as the Court is usually inclined to do with statutes that touch upon First Amendment interests.

It is quite clear, moreover, that the Court had a choice about how to interpret the statute before it. The relevant language of the statute—referring as it does to "communication by wire"—is not conclusive on the matter of commission jurisdiction over cable. It was also conceded by all concerned that Congress did not intend every type of wire communication to be covered (e.g., press services employ wire communication but are not subject to regulation). The issue, therefore, demanded an examination of such other factors as what special characteristics of a medium might justify regulation. The absence of such an examination recalls the Court's initial response to broadcast regulation some twenty-five years before in the *NBC* decision.

The Court's message of administrative encouragement in *Southwestern Cable* was not lost upon the commission. It proceeded with a policy of expanding its regulatory grip. A new rule required cable systems to develop their own programming, the so-called program origination rule.[49] This was challenged by one cable system in a case that came before the Supreme Court as *United States v. Midwest Video Corp. (I)*.[50] The FCC's position was straightforward and simple. It identified a longstanding policy—the promotion of outlets for local expression—and claimed that its program origination rule had been adopted in furtherance of that policy. There was irony in this argument, since the effect of the new rule might well be a reduction in the market of existing local broadcasters, the very threat that the commission had raised a few years earlier to justify its regulatory intervention into cable expansion. Now its position was that "a loss of audience or advertising revenue to a television station is not in itself a matter of moment to the public interest unless the result is a net loss of television service."[51]

The cable company's response in the case was to argue that the program origination rule represented a drastic extension of the regulatory authority approved in *Southwestern Cable*. Now, said the company, the commission was not acting merely to "protect" the market of local broadcasters against cable activities but was treating cable systems as subjects within the commission's domain which could be affirmatively ordered to do anything the agency felt would advance the "public interest."[52] The distinction violated, in other words, was one between *protection* of agency goals and *affirmative* implementation of those goals.

A majority of the Court rejected the cable company's position, though the justices overall were in some disagreement. The plurality opinion, written by Justice Brennan, portrayed the case as straightforward and simple, just as the FCC argued it was. "[W]e must agree with the Commission," he wrote, "that its concern with CATV carriage of broadcast signals is not just a matter of avoidance of adverse effects, but extends also to requiring CATV affirmatively to further statutory policies. . . . Since the avoidance of adverse effects is itself the furtherance of statutory policies, no sensible distinction even in theory can be drawn along those lines."[53]

To these justices the paramount need was for flexibility in the government's dealings with a "dynamic" new medium. With respect to the particular regulation at hand, the plurality found that the commission had met its burden by establishing a link between one of its longstanding goals (that of encouraging local self-expression) and the challenged regulation.

Chief Justice Burger concurred in the holding of the majority, but also stated that in his view this ruling strained the outer limit of regulatory intervention.[54] A dissenting opinion by Justice Douglas and three others argued that by the terms of the statute no authority was granted to compel people to become broadcasters, which they saw as the net effect of the program origination rule.[55]

The *Midwest Video I* decision was significant for the range of support it offered to the practice of government regulation of the electronic media. The term "electronic media" is used purposefully here, for the decision represented, I think, an important shift in constitutional thinking: from allowance of a regulatory system for *broadcasting* to allowance of such a system for the *electronic medium as a whole*. Yet this shift, even though important, was taken almost lightly. In the upside-down world of Supreme Court mass media decisions, we find that those justices who most typically, and solemnly, insist upon a strict separation of press and government now bear the flag on behalf of government intervention. Their evident enthusiasm for public regulation is conveyed in the language, the idiom, and the logic utilized to support the results. The almost totally uncritical posture is reflected in the weakness of the arguments they employ. Thus we find in Brennan's linguistic legerdemain the claim that no distinction can be drawn between regulations that "protect" and those that "affirmatively advance" commission goals. This is justified on the dubious ground that "protection" is itself a form of "advancement," clearly a failure to recognize that regulations may "advance" agency aims in different ways and that those differences may matter very greatly to us.[56] In *Midwest Video*, we find that, instead of an attitude of cautious endorsement of regulation, with critical scrutiny of government arguments in the light of traditional general principles, the Court employed precisely the opposite approach.

A few years later signs of reassessment appeared. In 1979, the Supreme Court decided *FCC v. Midwest Video Corp. (II)*,[57] another case contesting commission rules mandating public access to cable systems. Under these rules, all systems with subscribers above a specified number were required to have a minimum capacity of twenty channels and to reserve four of them for use by lessees, local government, educational systems, and the public. The cable operator was denied all control over these public access and leased channels, which were to be made available on a nondiscriminatory first-come, first-served basis.[58] Although the Court was split again, this time those who had prevailed in *Midwest Video I* were in dissent. A majority, drawing upon the reasoning of the *Columbia Broadcasting System v. Democratic National Committee* decision, argued that regulations divesting the cable operator of all control over the use of channels are impermissible under the statute. The precise grounds for that interpretation were left unclear. As with the *CBS* opinion, there is frequent reference to, and apparently great reliance placed upon, one of the definitional sections of the Communications Act (section 3[h]), which in effect states that broadcasters are not to be treated as "common carriers" under the statute.[59] Assuming that Congress intended this section to function as a source of substantive limitation on the agency's regulatory authority (a matter debated in the case), it remains unclear just what sort of regulatory behavior constitutes treatment of a broadcaster as a "common carrier." In *Southwestern* the Court had sharply refused to infer from congressional *inaction* on various proposals to amend the Communications Act any legislative intention to grant the commission jurisdiction over cable, on the view that discerning reasons for inaction is far more treacherous than determining why Congress enacted a piece of legislation. In *Midwest Video II*, however, the fact that Congress had rejected or neglected a variety of proposals for mandated access rules was seized upon as evincing a congressional intention, in 1927, to forever forbid any similar regulations. But neither the language of the section nor legislative history pointed to any clear idea of the limits of regulation. Here, for the first time in the cable area, the Court's majority opinion introduced the notion of cable operators possessing a cognizable *journalistic* interest, as exercising a form of "editorial discretion."[60] The introduction of this concept in connection with cable technology was striking. In a footnote the majority even intimated that First Amendment considerations had influenced its interpretation of the statute, stating, with pregnant implication, that the First Amendment "did not determine or sharply influence our construction of the statute."[61]

No doubt the commission must have felt it had been misled. Following upon the patterns laid down in *Southwestern* and *Midwest Video I*, the commission had come into court prepared to explain how the access rules were reasonable implementations of its longstanding policies of encouraging local self-expression and diversity of programming. In all likelihood, it confidently, and reasonably, expected a reception as warm as it had enjoyed in the past. Section 3(h) was hardly a formidable barrier, and, given the Court's history of considering the "dynamic" nature of the medium and the concomitant need for preserving a wide degree of "administrative flexibility," one would have expected it to interpret the provision narrowly, prohibiting only forms of regulation so extreme that they would convert broadcasters into the equivalent of the telephone system. Moreover, there was little reason to think that these access rules differed materially from, say, the program origination rule. Since the cable operator exerted no control over content, and the government had no role to play other than seeing that the channels were made available, this access system seemed to present far fewer problems of the kind generally associated with government supervision of content.

Here, then, is another tentative movement toward at least partially linking new technologies or media with traditional principles. Exactly how that is done, where the line is drawn between permissible and impermissible regulation, is worthy of significant attention and study. But one comes away from a line of cases like *Southwestern Cable* to *Midwest Video II* with larger questions in mind, and suspecting that a particular regulatory issue is seized upon less for its intrinsic importance than as an opportunity to maintain a way of thinking, or to spark a conceptual reevaluation of a new communications technology.

There is a contemporary sequel to this story of cable regulation and the principle of freedom of the press. Subsequent to the Court's decision in *Midwest Video II,* Congress enacted an extensive statute governing the regulation of cable. The issue of public access channels was specifically addressed and left to the discretion of states and local communities to decide whether to impose them.[62] Of course, many communities do. It remains to be seen what posture the Supreme Court will take toward cable regulation, and public access rules in particular. In 1986 a case came before the Court in which a cable operator objected to a decision by the City of Los Angeles to limit the number of cable operators in any given area to a single franchisee.[63] The argument was that, for First Amendment purposes, cable is more like a newspaper than a broadcaster. Since the case had been dismissed on a motion for summary judgment, the only question before the Court was whether, taking the facts as alleged by the cable company as true, they stated a plausible First Amendment claim. On this rather abstractly posed issue, the Court was quite clear, declaring explicitly that cable is indeed a medium with some First Amendment status. The case was sent back for trial, with the First Amendment issues more intensified but still ambiguous.[64]

Here, again, we see in this history a gradual evolution in thinking about the status of a new technology within the concept of freedom of the press. The Court has played a cautious role, slowly absorbing cable technology into the language and principles of a free press. The press community has been cautious, too, as evidenced by the fact that only in recent cases have the print or broadcast media filed briefs supporting or advancing claims on behalf of cable litigants.[65]

This chapter has explored the relationship between law, including administrative regulation as well as the constitutional principle of freedom of the press, and the development of the character of the American press. Clearly, the extent and nature of this relationship deserves further study. But it should be borne in mind that the idea that the state will play a role in shaping the character of the media is not entirely novel in the American system. Indeed, one of the explicit purposes behind the establishment of the system of public broadcasting was that it would provide a model, and through that an influence, for commercial television as well.[66] It is interesting to read the well-known Report of the Carnegie Commission on Educational Television, published in 1967, and the intellectual foundation for the Public Broadcasting Act of that same year, and to see how closely in their aspirations for the press they match the vision of the Hutchins commission two decades earlier.[67]

CHAPTER SIX

Reflections

Considering all this, in which ways should the law move? I have a number of answers and proposals for that question, which I offer here and in the next chapter. Virtually all of them spring from a belief that law at both the legislative and constitutional levels must be more prepared to focus on the *quality* of public discussion and decision making. It is not enough to conceive of the policies and values underlying the principle of freedom of the press only in terms of widening the stream of public debate, so that more information can flow to and among citizens. That is the image of *Sullivan,* and of Harry Kalven's final commentary on it, as was demonstrated in Chapter 1. Given the current character of constitutional law, and the directions in which it seems to be moving, this deeper inquiry—beyond quantity and into quality—is inescapable. It can also be, in my judgment, a good thing.

I

An appropriate place to begin is with the issues that closed Chapter 5, namely, the general question of the differential treatment of print and electronic media. We have seen that this is a difficult and complex development in the evolution of the principle of freedom of the press. Problems of theory are compounded by the difficulties of making sense out of what at first glance appears to be rather strange behavior. One is enmeshed in a web of historical circumstances that are hard to untangle, though untangling them is critical in deciding in which directions the law should move.

Two major issues must be faced. The first is how to think about the reasonableness of differential treatment, both as a matter of public policy and as a matter of First Amendment law. The second is how to evaluate the costs and benefits, in terms of the quality of public debate, of the various forms of public regulation of the media.

More than a decade ago, I proposed that the dual system of the press as it has evolved during this century, with unregulated print media and regulated electronic media, makes good sense in terms of both public policy and First Amendment theory.[1] I attempted to shift the debate from the course it had heretofore taken, in which the primary issue was always assumed to be whether broadcasting *differs* from the print media in ways relevant to the asserted need for public regulation. Instead, I argued, it is rational to treat the two branches of the media differently, even though they might be considered comparable, or similar, for such purposes. I called this a theory of partial regulation. Here, with minor editing, is what I argued:

Ultimately, the Court's decisions on the question of access regulation exhibit fundamental good sense. The good sense, however, derives not from the Court's treatment of broadcasting as being somehow special but rather from its apparent desire to limit the overall reach of access regulation. The Court need not, however, isolate the electronic media to achieve this result. Although it is uncertain whether the Court in *Miami Herald* saw it as such, the critical difference between what the Court was asked to do in *Red Lion* and what it was asked to do in *Miami Herald* involved choosing between a partial regulatory system and a universal one. Viewed from that perspective, the Court reached the correct result in both cases.

The central problem in this area results from the complexity of the access issue. The truth of the matter is, as the Court's opinions so plainly, if unintentionally, demonstrate, that there are good First Amendment reasons for being both receptive to and wary of access regulation. This dual nature of access legislation suggests the need to limit carefully the intrusiveness of the regulation in order safely to enjoy its remedial benefits. Thus, a proper judicial response is one that will permit the legislature to provide the public with access *somewhere* within the mass media but not throughout the press. The Court should not, and need not, be forced into an all-or-nothing position on this matter; there is nothing in the First Amendment that forbids having the best of both worlds.

Access regulation both responds to constitutional traditions and cuts against them. On the one hand, it helps to make possible the realization of First Amendment goals. Unlike attempts to censor types of speech, an access rule is designed to operate in the service of the First Amendment. It seeks to neutralize the disparities that impede the proper functioning of the "marketplace of ideas," to equalize opportunities within our society to command an audience and thereby to mobilize public opinion, and in that sense to help realize democratic ideals.

That unrestrained private interests can, at times, hamper the free exchange of ideas as seriously as governmental censorship has been apparent with painful clarity within the past half-century. Chafee wrote several decades ago about the need to define a new theoretical structure for governmental involvement in the implementation of First Amendment rights in response to the problems of private censorship:

> [W]hat is the use of telling an unpopular speaker that he will incur no criminal penalties by his proposed address, so long as every hall owner in the city declines to rent him space for his meetings and there are no vacant lots available? There should be municipal auditoriums, school-houses out of school hours, church forums, parks in summer, all open to thresh out every question of public importance, with just as few restrictions as possible; for otherwise the subjects that most need to be discussed will be the very subjects that will be ruled out as unsuitable for discussion.
>
> We must do more than remove the discouragements to open discussion. We must exert ourselves to supply active encouragement.[2]

Chafee's articulation of the seeds of an "affirmative" theory of freedom of speech constituted an important qualification of the thinking of laissez-faire theorists such as John Stuart Mill and John Milton. Many commentators since Chafee have elaborated on his idea.[3] The debate that has been generated unquestionably involves one of the most vital First Amendment issues of our time.

The Supreme Court has, through its actions, occasionally demonstrated that it recognizes the serious problems posed by unregulated private interests operating in areas that affect the First Amendment. In a seminal decision in *Associated Press v. United States*,[4] the Court approved a governmental order directing a national wire service to make its news available on a nondiscriminatory basis, stating that "[f]reedom of the press from governmental interference under the first amendment does not sanction repression of that freedom by private interests."[5] In another well-known line of cases, the Court held that a private company town and a shopping center were prohibited under the First Amendment from excluding certain speech that the private owners would have preferred to censor.[6] These decisions, together with *Red Lion*, outline a still tentative approach to removing the inequalities in speech opportunities.[7]

Of all the efforts thus far to restructure private arrangements that impinge on the "marketplace of ideas," however, access regulation represents the most direct assault and, consequently, the most dangerous.[8] Although its aims conform to those of the First Amendment, the methods of access regulation constitute a significant departure from our traditional constitutional notions concerning the need to maintain a distance between the government and the press, especially on matters directly touching news content. Access regulation carries the greatest potential for altering the press as we have known it and for exposing us to grave risks.

In general, access regulation may have three adverse consequences for the marketplace of ideas. The first is its most commonly identified cost: access regulation may have a depressing effect on journalistic motivation to engage in discourse on social issues.[9] This cost is presumably greater with some forms of access regulation than with others. The chilling effect associated with right-of-reply rules, for example, is likely to be much greater than that associated with the requirement that editors publish advertisements on a nondiscriminatory basis. Even where the chilling effect is thought to be a problem, however, no data exist on the extent to which regulation is inhibiting. Nevertheless, in cases in which a significant chilling effect may predictably occur, there is cause for concern given society's general commitment to the idea that debate is most likely to be fruitful if it is "uninhibited, robust, and wide-open."[10] The prospect that some regulated editors will forgo coverage of some political discussion because of reply requirements need not necessitate rejection of access regulation, for the benefits may still outweigh this cost. Such a cost, however, remains a matter of concern and should be minimized as much as possible.

A second general concern associated with access regulation involves the risk that the administrative machinery required to implement it will be used to force the press into some official line, thereby undermining its role as a critic and antagonist of government. The potential for official misbehavior has been a traditional reason for withholding approval of governmental schemes to "improve" the press.[11] It is a consideration that is reflected in the sum of our experience and should not be lightly disregarded. Evidence that this risk is still vital may, regrettably, be found in an examination of the presidential politics of Watergate.

In the course of the revelations about Watergate, it was learned that the executive branch, angered by unflattering remarks and disclosures of government secrets, embarked on an intensive campaign to harass the press. A substantial part of the attack apparently involved using administrative machinery to apply pressure on journalists.[12] There were also allegations that the executive branch sought to harass the Washington Post by creating difficulties for its subsidiary radio stations with the Federal Communications Commission.[13] If there is a First Amendment lesson in Watergate, it is that we should continue to be wary of making official machinery available for the regulation of the press. A regulatory structure stands as a constant temptation to government officials—a source of leverage with which to compel obedience within the press and, in more subtle ways, to manipulate the content of public debate.

The third potential adverse consequence of access regulation is that it may result in an escalation of press restrictions, the camel's-nose-in-the-tent argument. This criticism is one of those stock arguments that suffers badly from overuse. It is easy to dismiss the claim because it is advanced so often in circumstances where it carries no conviction. With respect to access regulation, however, the argument has powerful force and should not go unheeded. The problem is not simply that regulation will induce irresistible pressure for censorship. The dangers are more subtle and complicated. Access regulation comes in a variety of shapes and sizes. Some forms, such as a vigorously enforced fairness doctrine, can lead to utter blandness of content and in this way may permit official manipulation of the news. In addition, it is virtually impossible for the Court to articulate unambiguous standards in advance. Experience with a particular regulation will often be necessary to judge its desirability and constitutionality. It is important to know, for example, how frequently the government will be drawn into conflict with editors,[14] what financial burdens administrative procedures will impose on those regulated, and whether the administering officials will be prone to misconduct or will exhibit a healthy respect for First Amendment freedoms.[15]

By sanctioning the concept of access regulation, the Court can expect administrative experimentation with various types of regulation. And, since clear guidelines cannot be established, there may be constant pressure to expand the regulatory power into impermissible areas. The clamor for greater regulation may itself be used as a weapon to bend the press into line. If what turns out to be an improper regulation is imposed, irremediable harm may occur before the Court can act. Similarly, the difficulty of assessing the future consequences of a regulation may lead the Court to sanction conduct that is ultimately very harmful.[16] It must be remembered that "[l]egal experiments, once started, cannot be stopped the moment they show signs of working badly."[17]

Viewed in its entirety, therefore, access regulation is both desirable and dangerous. That it raises a constitutional problem of enormous difficulty is reflected in the seemingly schizophrenic decisions of *Red Lion* and *Miami Herald*. But sometimes wisdom hides in the garb of pathology. In light of the double-edged character of access regulation, and the special circumstances of the mass media, it may make sense to affirm congressional authority to implement a regulatory scheme, but only partially within the media. With this approach, with a major branch of the press remaining free of regulation, the costs and risks of regulation may be held at an acceptable level. Expressed another way, only under such a system can we afford to allow the degree of governmental regulation that is necessary to realize the objectives of public access.

One advantage of a partial regulatory system is that the unregulated sector provides an effective check against each of the costs of regulation. A partial scheme offers some assurance that information not disseminated by the regulated sector will nevertheless be published by the unregulated press. If, for example, a broadcast station chooses not to cover a debate between mayoral candidates because of equal time obligations, then the public will still be informed of the event by the local newspaper. A partial scheme also offers some assurance that government abuse of regulatory authority to bludgeon the press into an official line will not suppress the truth. If, for example, the Washington Post had curtailed its Watergate investigation to ward off what might reasonably have been perceived as government pressure on its radio stations, other newspapers free of government entanglements, such as the New York Times, would almost certainly have continued the investigation. Finally, such a system gives some assurance that the pressures for and effects of harmful regulation will be cushioned. If, for example, a vice-president were to urge more vigorous access regulation in order to ward off criticism of the president (as Vice-President Spiro Agnew arguably did during the Nixon administration), and if the regulated sector complied, the unregulated press would remain active.

Restricting regulation to only a part of the press offers more than a check against these costs. It also provides a beneficial tension within the system. The unregulated sector can operate to minimize all three costs of regulation. Consider, for example, the chilling effect problem. The publication of news in the unregulated media serves as a competitive prod to the regulated press to publish what it might otherwise omit.[18] Thus, while broadcasters may initially have been reluctant to cover

Watergate events, because of fears of official reprisals and access obligations, a decision not to cover the story became impossible once the print media began exploiting it.[19]

The most significant aspect of a partial scheme, however, is that it preserves a benchmark—an important link to our constitutional traditions—as the Court permits experimentation with regulation. The continuing link to traditional First Amendment theory conveys the message that old principles have not been abandoned, and it forces every departure to be carefully scrutinized and justified. The message is one of adjustment rather than wholesale revision.[20]

It is worth noting, again, that one of the more interesting features of the broadcast regulation experience has been the absence of egregious abuses by the FCC. The commission has, on the whole, been extraordinarily circumspect in the exercise of its powers.[21] This self-restraint may be explained in large part by the juxtaposition of the autonomous print media, representing continued respect for the ideal of a free press, against the regulated broadcast media. By preserving the unregulated print media, the benchmark against which reform must continually be measured, even if not explicitly, the Court has furnished a built-in restraint against regulatory excesses. Because representatives of broadcasters have been able to point to the print media as a concrete embodiment of traditional constitutional principles, rather than having to resort to a mere abstract principle of freedom of the press, every regulation must be justified as a departure. The effect of this process can be readily observed in such court decisions as *Columbia Broadcasting System v. Democratic National Committee* and *National Broadcasting Co. v. FCC* (the *Pensions* case), where frequent references to the print media demonstrate the force of the newspaper analogy.[22]

In an article on broadcast regulation written in 1967, Harry Kalven observed that "[l]aw . . . is determined by a choice between competing analogies."[23] What had been "sorely needed" in the broadcasting area, he suggested, was "the competing analogy to set against the claims for control,"[24] for there had never been "a precedent setting the *outer boundaries* of [FCC] control."[25] While the absence of an explicit limit on commission authority is unfortunate, it has not been problematic precisely because the unregulated print media has provided a "competing analogy."

From this perspective, the *Miami Herald* decision begins to make sense. On the surface, it seems singularly inattentive to parallel broadcasting cases, yet in fact it speaks directly to them. *Red Lion* had given the impression that editorial rights are subordinate to the "public's right to hear." This spawned a political and legal movement, spearheaded by Professor Barron,[26] plaintiff's counsel in *Miami Herald,* for more extensive regulation. In its reaffirmation of fundamental First Amendment principles, the Court's opinion in *Miami Herald* urges caution and restraint and sharply limits regulatory reform. Although the opinion still does not rate high on the scale of judicial craftsmanship, it is nevertheless explicable.

This analysis of *Red Lion* and *Miami Herald* demonstrates the need to maintain a partial regulatory structure *for its own sake.* What the Court has never fully appreciated is that the very similarity of the two major branches of the mass media provides a rationale for treating them differently. By permitting differential treatment of these institutions, the Court can promote realization of the benefits of two distinct constitutional values, both of which ought to be fostered: access in a highly concentrated press and minimal government intervention. Thus neither side of the access controversy emerges victorious. The Court has imposed a compromise, not based on notions of expedience but on a reasoned, principled, accommodation of competing First Amendment values.

II

After fifteen years, I remain attracted to the partial regulation thesis as the best means of understanding both the rationale for and the nature of the system of the press freedom that has evolved during this century. Over time the benefits of acting in this divided way have only become clearer to me.

There is a sound intellectual theory that justifies proceeding in this fashion. A society, like an individual, may be ambivalent, or uncertain, about how to organize itself. It is often difficult to imagine what life will be like if certain choices are made or traditions departed from. When this occurs, it is sensible to experiment with alternatives, and to live them as fully, and as *purely,* as possible. In an important sense, this is a simple extension of the cognitive theory of the First Amendment premise developed earlier, that unreserved commitment to belief has its advantages in the search for truth. Unmodified belief (encouraged, at least implicitly, by opinions like *New York Times v. Sullivan*) is good when it causes us to dig deeper. And so a divided system has the great advantage of permitting experimentation and the manifestation of ambivalence.

Like many people, as I reflect upon the prospect of a completely autonomous press and one with some public accountability, I find myself deeply ambivalent—ambivalent, it should be said, using First Amendment values as the relevant guide. There is, as I argue in Chapter 3, something deeply noble about the idea of a press that is almost entirely free and independent of public regulation. There may well be a spirit to such a press that cannot exist in any other system. If modified, it is destroyed. On the other hand, public debate in a democracy has become too critical a matter to leave access in the hands of a few people whose interests may be inconsistent with those of good decision making. If judges were to say, "Trust us, we wish to stop writing opinions explaining what we do," we would properly answer, "We can't." If "only a few people" control access, thus possessing the power to thwart good decision making, then some means of public accountability seems desirable. But, in the end, it may only be possible to express ambivalent feelings about which course to follow. The issue then becomes whether an ambivalent response is justifiable.

To some people, a system manifesting ambivalence appears to violate the virtue of "consistency." But that conclusion merits further reflection. Few people have trouble with the idea that *legislatures* often address only a portion of a general problem. Perhaps it is natural to wonder whether drawing a line that treats broadcasters differently from print journalists constitutes improper "discrimination," or a violation of the principle of equality. But that ought not to be a deep concern. Differential treatment reflects no animus toward broadcasters; nor is there social inferiority either created or reinforced by the selection of broad-casting as the medium with which to insure a fuller discussion of public issues. The regulations, moreover, are not something a broadcaster cannot entirely escape should it prove personally humiliating. And, in general, it is not uncommon in society for some—that is to say, fewer than all—to be chosen to bear the burdens of needed, but only partial, reforms.

The issue of consistency seems to arise most often at the level of constitutional theory. Somehow, without saying why, it is thought that, while Congress may legitimately choose to reg-ulate one medium because of the greater net benefits of a partial regime, it is inappropriate for the First Amendment to instruct Congress that it can choose only to regulate one. The Consti-tution, this notion continues, ought to be a general principle: either Congress can regulate, in which case it can regulate all or part, or it can't, in which case no part of the media can be regulated.

This self-imposed limitation on First Amendment options is unduly fastidious, for it is important not to be intellectually crippled by the charge of inconsistency. To be consistent should mean that we do only what we have good reasons for doing, that we act in a way "consistent" with our reasoned wants and de-sires. Sometimes this means that we treat things similarly for some, or perhaps all, purposes. But it would be a crazy world indeed if one felt compelled to treat everything the same. The critical issue is, as it always has been, determining what one wants and ought to want.

There are further advantages to a divided approach. Recall from our previous discussion of the Hutchins commission report the suggestion, offered only in passing: "An ideal combination would include general media, inevitably solicitous to present their own views, but setting forth other views fairly. As checks on their fairness, and partial safeguards against ignoring impor-tant matters, more specialized media of advocacy have a vital place."[27] This reflects two concepts well worth thinking about. One is the value of mixed systems in yielding the most infor-mation, which is what lies behind the notion of partial regula-tion. The second is more complex.

Even if there were many and diverse media available within

the society, one still might wish to have some medium representing, or manifesting, a principle of fairness. I do not mean to raise the frequently heard, but not trivial, alarm about the proliferation of media options—primarily through cable—causing the society to suffer because citizens will not share a common source of information. I want to sketch a different point, one best represented by the image of the trial.

Earlier, in discussing a revisionist interpretation of the autonomy approach, I argued that an adversarial system holds within it important advantages for the exploration of ideas. Unmodified belief, encouraged by opinions like *New York Times v. Sullivan,* is good where it encourages people to probe more deeply. The commission report properly upholds the importance of this idea. But belief can also be self-blinding. You may dig deeper at the cost of foreshortening your vision. In a trial, there are advocates, each representing a position, but there is also an impartial judge (or jury) who ultimately decides. A world filled with advocates would be a terrible thing; so would a world of judges.

I have, therefore, this further hypothesis: that the media, in addition to their role as sources of information, also represent important intellectual styles. Some are cast in the model of advocates, some in the model of judges. The fairness doctrine does not forbid broadcasters from expressing points of view, even fiercely if they want; it only tells them that, if they do, they must ensure that the opposing view is expressed as well. But here we may draw upon the profound modern insight that the medium is the message.[28] And one of the most significant effects of public regulations such as the fairness doctrine is the transmission of a message about a valued intellectual trait. The regulated medium itself becomes an intellectual type, one we need, just as an advocacy newspaper is a much-needed intellectual type. Public regulation thus has the benefit not only of offering access to ideas and voices otherwise excluded or disadvantaged in public debate but of reinforcing a desired intellectual style. But if one accepts that view, further thought must be given to a thesis I put forward earlier—namely, that one of the advantages of public regulation is that it is a way to instruct other branches of the media (i.e., print) in proper journalistic standards. By the present view, that approach may go too far and undermine the goal of encouraging the development of a rich mix of intellectual styles within the overall media.

III

One must also be careful not to assume that the process of identifying advantages is the same as the process of deciding what should be done. Many difficult issues remain to be considered. A system of partial regulation, for example, may be foolish in a world of extensive cross-ownership between newspapers and broadcasters;[29] or, in a world, which some foresee, of near total domination by the electronic medium.[30] And, to the extent that the value of a partial regulation scheme depends upon it affecting the marketplace of ideas as a whole, we must determine how many people read or view only *unregulated* media or are otherwise untouched by the regulations.[31] Moreover, I have now moved away from a position I took initially that a system of partial regulation could be applied to any portion of the media. In theory that would mean the government could decide to shift from regulation of broadcasting to regulation of newspapers. I now believe that there are special advantages to limiting regulation to new technologies, advantages having to do with the importance of the different social perceptions that seem to attach to traditional (print) and newer (electronic) media. The psychological value of maintaining print as a benchmark, the place where press freedom was born and has flourished, seems more powerful to me today than it did some years ago. But that remains a central issue.

I have already indicated that public regulation of broadcasting is now under strong attack and may even be fighting for its life. Opposition to regulation, which has been gradually gaining strength over the last decade, now has such force that even the FCC, the very federal agency that developed the principal regulations at issue and has served as overseer of the system for the past half-century, is openly calling for a return to the free market system as the exclusive mechanism for ensuring a rich marketplace of ideas. That politics makes strange bedfellows has long been appreciated, but the alliance of political ideologies that stands behind opposition to public regulation gives new life to that ancient adage. The commission's 1985 "Report on the General Fairness Doctrine Obligations of Broadcast Licensees,"[32] which first issued the call for the abandonment of the fairness doctrine, draws heavily on the general First Amendment opinions of Justice William O. Douglas (who, ironically, long supported broadcast regulation).

Indeed, the fairness doctrine is now the primary battleground for the war being waged over public regulation of the media. Generally, three arguments are leveled against it. First, it is claimed that the doctrine chills more speech than it fosters. Because it imposes a variety of costs on broadcasters—such as the cost of covering opposing viewpoints at the licensee's own expense and the cost of resisting fairness doctrine complaints— broadcasters often decline to cover public issues at all, thus reducing instead of expanding the amount of discussion of public issues. Second, it is said that the doctrine is unenforceable in any principled way because a decision as to what is and what is not a "controversial issue of public importance," and whether a given broadcaster's programming has provided only one side of an issue, is fundamentally "subjective," inevitably leading to inconsistent decisions based on unarticulated premises.[33] Finally, and most important, it is claimed that the fairness doctrine must be repealed because the rationale behind it has disappeared. Increased opportunities for entry into both the electronic and print media, it is said, have destroyed the old oligopolistic market, making it possible to rely on the free market as the sole method of allocation for political information and ideas.

Together these three arguments constitute the principal contemporary case against the fairness doctrine, and they enjoy a forceful as well as an official articulation in the commission's 1985 report. But these arguments, at least as they have been developed by the current opponents of public regulation, are seriously flawed. In many respects, I would say, they even do a disservice to thoughtful reconsideration of the wisdom of public regulation.

The issue at the moment is *not* whether the fairness doctrine has in fact yielded a net gain, compared to other alternatives, when measured by the goal of achieving good public debate. Rather, the primary concern is how we should *think* about that question as we set about deciding what course to follow in the future. Our methods of evaluation deserve further scrutiny. Here I want to offer responses to two of the three criticisms of the fairness doctrine noted above, leaving the discussion of whether a free market dispels the need for public intervention until the next chapter.

First, consider the claim of the inherent unenforceability of the fairness doctrine. Looking back over the case law of the past few decades, one finds a number of highly controverted decisions, with commissioners and judges disagreeing about various aspects of the doctrine, unable to give convincing reasons for their views, and frequently reversing themselves over time. We have seen how, in a series of cases beginning in the late 1960s, the commission proceeded from requiring broadcasters who aired cigarette commercials to provide airtime for antismoking messages, to considering a number of fairness doctrine complaints about other commercial advertisements—which produced split results—to its 1974 position of virtually conceding error in having followed the fairness doctrine into the commercial thicket.[34] We also saw how in the *Pensions* case the federal court of appeals was severely split on the question whether an NBC documentary on abuses in pension programs was about "some abuses in some programs" (a noncontroversial proposition) or an implicit assertion that the pension system was badly in need of significant legislative reform (a highly controversial issue).[35] After pages of judicial argument about the meaning of the text of the program, the case was eventually dismissed as moot.

To some people, this record demonstrates that the fairness doctrine is unenforceable, in accordance with the usual standards of principled decision making. The doctrine requires balanced coverage of "controversial issues of public importance." But what "issue," or "issues," does any given program address? If the doctrine is applied only to the "explicit" message of a program, some clarity of assessment is achieved—but only at the expense of providing an opportunity for evasion so vast as to render the doctrine useless. On the other hand, if subtle expressions of viewpoint are considered relevant, the result is a doctrine with bite but one that also requires a hopelessly "subjective" evaluation of the real impact of a program on its audience. Furthermore, because the doctrine applies only to issues of "public importance," government as well as the courts are inevitably drawn into making judgments about which issues are most important—and that, it is argued, is something the First Amendment does not allow.

Much can be said about this line of argument (especially about the difficulties of establishing workable guiding principles for any new area of law), but one simple point puts the issue in proper perspective: the fairness doctrine is no more open-ended, no more vulnerable to unprincipled, "subjective" decisions, and no more dependent on the development of a hierarchy of values in the realm of public issues than are other well-established areas of First Amendment jurisprudence. In the libel area, for example, we now face similar tasks of deciding, in public figure cases, what controversies warrant the most uninhibited debate and, on the matter of distinguishing statements of opinion from statements of fact, what the overall impact is on the general audience. Uncertainty and the need to reach difficult judgments are hardly unique to public access regulations such as the fairness doctrine.

To my mind, these cases seem like admirable first efforts aimed at developing more sophisticated notions about what actually happens in discussions about public issues. That confusion and uncertainty about the issues featured prominently in all of them is, I think, undeniable. Much of this stemmed from the reluctance of judges to meddle in questions of how we come by the central images that affect what we believe and how we vote. That inconsistent decisions resulted seems inevitable, yet unimportant. The issues raised in the cases were novel, with powerful First Amendment considerations cutting both ways—the interest in having the government, including the courts, respect press freedom, and the interest of society in improving the quality of public debate. The latter interest will, if followed without caution, push any decision maker into deeper and deeper analysis of the publication in question and of the mind that listened to or watched it. It will rarely be easy to ascertain the influence of a given program. On the other hand, that is knowledge it would be nice to have. The fact that the short-term results of cases dealing with the issues were inconsistent decisions should be neither unexpected nor threatening to the future of the fairness doctrine, anymore than one would consider abolishing the First Amendment because there have been so many inconsistent interpretations of the "clear and present danger" exception. Mistakes of this sort are merely costs that have to be weighed against the importance placed on the public good an amendment, or a doctrine, is capable of bringing. With respect to the fairness doctrine, the mistakes may also be attributed to the special atmosphere of the time in which judges were uncomfortable with the kind of inquiry the fairness doctrine demanded they undertake.

The second argument against the fairness doctrine claims that it actually functions to discourage discussion of public issues. It is, indeed, vitally important that such regulations be assessed to determine how well they really work. For this, the American experience of the past half-century constitutes a kind of national treasure. In the late 1940s, when Zechariah Chafee (as a member of the Hutchins commission) considered the idea of using public institutions to improve the quality of the press, he treated the proposal as a wholly abstract inquiry. "[W]e are," he began, "in almost unexplored territory."[36] Apart from the system of public education, libraries, and museums, there was no practical experience upon which Chafee could call to help answer the question "what government can and should do affirmatively to improve the quality of the traffic in news and ideas."[37] Considering the FCC's contemporary report on the "Public Service Responsibility of Broadcast Licensees," which required broadcasters to carry programs devoted to the discussion of public issues, a proposal to create a state "Free Press Authority," which would administer a kind of fairness doctrine for all media, and a proposal for a system of subsidies to small communications organizations, Chafee responded by stressing the difficulties of anticipating the implications of abstract ideas.[38] "All we have," he began, "is some brief outlines of untried laws. Nobody has attempted to envisage all sorts of things which will happen when those laws are put into operation. Hence no convincing case is made for this far-reaching new legislation."[39]

Chafee supported this conclusion with several pages of speculations about how problems of quality in the media arise mostly from the audiences, whom law cannot change; about how the situation may not have been as deplorable as some suggested; about how legal solutions provide opportunities for biased or ignorant officials to implement their misperceptions; about how even sound and sensible legal solutions are undesirable when they encourage subsequent unsound solutions; and about how it is preferable to rely upon self-regulation and the efforts of private organizations to elevate public desires, with occasional supplemental government programs of public education (such as making fine literature, ideas, and art available through public libraries and museums).[40]

But these were mere speculations, entertained in an experiential vacuum. Today the situation is very different from what it was in Chafee's and the Hutchins commission's day. We have experimented with a variety of efforts to influence the quality of the mass media, and, though it is often a picture composed of the subtlest hues, it is important that the experience be treated with care. This remains true even if abandonment of public involvement with the media is the wiser choice at the moment, because it is important for society to record its experience for the distant as well as the near future. Unfortunately, that was not done by the commission in its 1985 report.

The weaknesses of the commission's finding that the fairness doctrine has an unacceptable chilling effect on coverage of public issues seem self-evident. Its conclusion rested entirely on acceptance of the testimonial claims of some broadcasters that they had chosen not to report on public issues out of a fear that such coverage would generate the costs of a fairness doctrine complaint.[41] The commission found these statements credible because they were considered to be statements against self-interest, given the professional embarrassment and risk of an adverse regulatory response attendant upon admitting that they, as broadcast licensees, had chosen not to fulfill their journalistic and legal obligations to cover political issues.[42] In a footnote, the commission rejected the possibility of using the first part of the fairness doctrine (which independently requires broadcasters to provide coverage of public issues) to overcome this inhibition, and its consequent chilling effect, on the grounds that such a course would "increase the government's intrusion into the editorial decisionmaking process of broadcast journalists," "enlarge the opportunity for governmental officials to abuse the doctrine for partisan political purposes," and "increase the economic costs that are borne both by broadcasters and the commission."[43]

This position, as developed and expressed by the commission, is insufficient. The credibility of the broadcasters' testimony seems far more open to doubt than the commission assumes. After all, a broadcaster who claims to have been chilled may have his or her professional embarrassment significantly reduced, if not eliminated, by the enhanced reputation that presumably would result from having challenged government regulation of journalism. Further, fear of retaliation by the agency surely must have been viewed as of marginal importance, given an awareness of the commission's unsympathetic predisposition to the fairness doctrine.

It must also be said that the commission only considered half of the real issue. For, even if the fairness doctrine has chilled in the instances asserted, we still must decide how much can be inferred from the concrete evidence about the overall level of chilling. This must be weighed, in turn, against instances in which the doctrine induces compliance, thereby increasing the number of voices that would exist without the doctrine. These inquiries the commission wholly ignored. Finally, as to the commission's dismissal of the possibility of enforcing the first part of the fairness doctrine (something the Supreme Court in *Red Lion* indicated was possible should broadcasters prove reluctant to cover controversial issues of public importance because of the costs associated with complying with the fairness doctrine),[44] it should be clear that the potential costs associated with that course cannot reasonably be regarded as decisive until we have considered the benefits of more rigorous enforcement.[45]

What we really need to know, and do not know yet, is what benefits we may hope to derive from regulations such as the fairness doctrine, and the extent to which that hope is realized in practice. One would like to know on how many occasions broadcasters are induced by the fairness doctrine to cover controversial issues and provide coverage of valuable points of view they would otherwise ignore. But, as the discussion in earlier chapters indicates, we should also wish to know to what extent the fairness doctrine plays an important symbolic role in other media, thereby shaping the behavior of journalists in desirable ways.

The intention here is not to defeat the position taken by the commission in its report but to indicate its general deficiencies and, further, demonstrate the need for other institutions to evaluate these important matters. The fairness doctrine may well be inadequate when compared to other alternatives. In its report the commission did not consider whether other forms of public regulation might work. From its initial decision that the costs of the fairness doctrine were serious, the commission jumped to the conclusion that all regulation must be jettisoned—repeating the common error that was the source of controversy in the *Pensions* case. There are many other alternatives, ranging from a requirement that time periods be set aside for public discussion on a first-come-first-served basis to a mandate requiring broadcast media to sell commercial airtime to individuals or groups wishing to debate public issues.

One drawback of the fairness doctrine has been that it has only required broadcasters to cover issues that are already controversial, which means that issues not yet in the mainstream of public debate can be (and generally are) excluded. The doctrine has also left the choice about coverage of viewpoints to the general discretion of the broadcaster, which means that strong dissenting voices have rarely been heard. This feature of the fairness doctrine produced at least one irony in the history of broadcast regulation. Recall the Supreme Court's decision in 1973, in *Columbia Broadcasting System v. Democratic National Committee,* in which the Court rejected the claim of a statutory and constitutional right to purchase airtime for the purpose of discussing public issues.[46] The Court's plurality opinion, while ostensibly rejecting this claim out of respect for the editorial and journalistic discretion of broadcasters (the first time, it will be remembered, the Court used those words in reference to broadcasters, and was for that reason hailed by them as a special victory), reflected a deeper motivation to preserve control over discussions of public issues in the hands of the broadcasters because they tend to favor inoffensive programming. One of the litigants in that case was a group called Business Executives Move for Vietnam Peace, which had been unable to buy airtime to show napalmed villages as part of its campaign of opposition to the war.

There can be no denying the fact that it is extremely difficult to evaluate the overall social benefits and costs of public regulations, just as it is extremely difficult to evaluate the effect of the Supreme Court's images of the press on the character of modern journalism. But to ignore considerations because they are hard to measure or to restrict artificially the scope of one's examination is to risk reaching unsound, even absurd, conclusions. Rules of public access, in whatever form they take, may to someone insensitive to the social context or to subtle influences seem to achieve nothing more than a waste of social resources for not a single identifiable gain. How many good ideas have come out of cable public access channels? one might ask. But if the same question were asked about Speaker's Corner in Hyde Park, one would think the questioner silly. Is the value to English society of that Hyde Park corner only to be measured in the number of interesting ideas that have emanated from that piece of urban parkland?

Cable public access is not Speaker's Corner in Hyde Park. But presumably this was not always what it is today either.[47] What does it take to create public symbols that represent for a society certain qualities of mind that it wishes to hold before itself to aspire to? That is a very difficult question. But it is also a vitally important question.

IV

In recent years, a number of scholarly works on the experience of broadcast regulation have appeared. One of the most comprehensive in its attempt to evaluate the performance of the government in that enterprise is Professor Scot Powe's *American Broadcasting and the First Amendment*.[48] In it Powe sets out to empirically assess what my own partial regulation theory dealt with only theoretically. Against the generally prevailing view that broadcast regulation has been afflicted with few abuses,[49] Powe argues that there have been many. He concludes his book with this statement:

> This book has been written against the background of Lee Bollinger's seminal thesis that a press half free and half tethered provides us both the uninhibited reaching and the balance necessary to serve First Amendment goals. This book, quite obviously, is my dissent. The evidence I have presented demonstrates that the licensed half of the press has been subject to political abuses wholly inconsistent with a concept of freedom of expression. I do not believe, therefore, that Bollinger's thesis can stand. At a minimum I believe the complacency of Bollinger's followers in the academy is unfounded.[50]

Powe's main thesis is that what might be called marginal, or radical, voices within the broadcast media have sometimes been penalized or even driven from the airwaves. In the early years of broadcast regulation, the commission refused to renew the license of one individual as a result of allegedly outrageous attacks on various persons, including public officials.[51] We have encountered Fred Friendly's discovery that the Democratic National Committee monitored right-wing broadcasts, an action supposedly intended to counteract conservative programming through the filing of fairness doctrine complaints (a system that led to the *Red Lion* case itself). Powe repeats this story.[52] There were also a number of cases in which the commission investigated or sanctioned stations, all of which were out of the mainstream, for "indecent" programs.[53]

Powe finds abuses with respect to mainstream broadcasters. He repeats a claim made in the late 1950s that television licenses were dispensed as political rewards,[54] and he devotes a chapter to describing the Nixon administration efforts to intimidate the press through Vice-President Agnew's speeches, through threats of monitoring public affairs programming for bias, and through legal challenges to the Washington Post's radio stations.[55] Finally, Powe argues that FCC commissioners have tended to favor the presidents who appointed them when access issues are at stake.[56]

Powe concludes by denying the legitimacy of any public regulation of the media: "Although I fully sympathize with the concerns of the 'newer First Amendment' advocates, I believe that the older First Amendment, which rejects an affirmative government role as being fundamentally inconsistent with an open democracy, has served us well and ought not to be discarded."[57] My reaction to Professor Powe's work is similar to that I expressed earlier with regard to the commission's 1985 report.

There are many reasons why Professor Powe's study fails to sustain his ultimate conclusion. First, he neglects to consider that identifying an abuse in the past may not be helpful in assessing the potential for abuses in the future. Powe, for example, may be right in claiming that the commission in 1932 improperly denied a license renewal to a station because of the political content of that station's editorializing. But it is not at all clear, indeed it would seem unlikely, that such an abuse would be repeated today when broadcast regulation has become much more sensitive to First Amendment values.

Second, not everything Powe identifies as an abuse may be such. Roosevelt may have wanted to forestall newspaper owners from becoming broadcast licensees for the wrong reason (i.e., because newspaper owners generally opposed his policies), but such a proposal is not inherently bad; indeed, a variation is in effect today and widely applauded for increasing diversity of media ownership.[58] Neither is it clear that establishing a system of monitoring right-wing broadcasts for purposes of making fairness doctrine claims is necessarily evil in its effects. After all, the purpose of the fairness doctrine is to provide balanced discussion of public issues, and it relies on listener complaints to achieve that goal.

Third, one must bear in mind the distinction between attempting an abuse and committing one. In the final analysis, Roosevelt failed to achieve his wish to foreclose newspapers from owning radio stations. Similarly, the Nixon administration efforts to intimidate the Washington Post, though quite real, were nevertheless quite unsuccessful. As Powe himself says, "Of course, none of this happened."[59] Powe also argues that these efforts caused the networks to subdue their criticism of the administration's actions and policies, but the evidence of that is very slight.[60]

Fourth, as we continue reviewing the system of public regulation of broadcasting, it is vital that the relationship between the types of abuses and the types of regulations be carefully matched. I agree, for example, that the commission and the courts, including the Supreme Court, have been insensitive to freedom of speech and press interests in the area of regulation of "indecent" language.[61] It is not at all clear, however, that this problem would have been avoided had there not been other regulations, such as the equal time rule or the fairness doctrine, or that one should expect similar insensitivity in the enforcement of these rules.

Fifth, even after one has identified relevant instances of abuse, we ought to consider first whether changes in the structure of regulation might eliminate the risk of future repetition. Professor Powe does not undertake that kind of inquiry. Once he finds that there have been some abuses, he immediately concludes that the entire regulatory system should be abolished. But surely there are more intermediate possibilities to consider. If, for example, presidents are unduly tempted to pressure commissioners into being biased in their favor, that risk might be diminished by further depoliticizing the appointment process or by lengthening the term of office for commissioners.

Sixth, and finally, Professor Powe errs in the same way as the commission's 1985 report. This whole matter of evaluating the success or failure of broadcast regulation must be considered on a larger scale. A study of abuses must be accompanied by a study of the benefits to public debate that public regulation has brought and can bring. For every instance in which public debate may have suffered because of public regulation, there may be ten cases like that involving WLBT, the Jackson, Mississippi, station owned by Lamar Broadcasting, whose license was stripped after years of presenting only a prosegregationist point of view and refusing to permit blacks, who constituted nearly half of its community, an opportunity to respond.[62] And, further, what counts as a benefit must also be more liberally understood. Finally, the analysis must in the end be comparative: without public regulation, what "abuses" will private media commit and thereby cause harm to full and fair public discussion of public issues.

Still, this contemporary effort to assay the experience of broadcast regulation, to study its character and behavior, is certainly to be applauded. That it is still too little, and comes rather late, should not prevent us from being grateful for what we have or from asking for more.

A New Image

The discussion over the past six chapters should, if nothing more, reveal that the American idea of freedom of the press, both in theory and in practice, must be regarded as significantly more complex than the central image portrayed by *New York Times v. Sullivan* and its progeny. Under that primitive image the goal of press freedom is viewed as the creation of a vast space for "uninhibited, robust, and wide-open" public discussion. It is further assumed that the role of the Supreme Court is to stand guard against government intervention, permitting it only when the public interest counters with an overwhelming competing interest to that of free and open debate. Examined critically, however, this posture seems insensitive to problems affecting the quality of public discussion that are posed by a laissez-faire system of modern mass media.

But the modern system has not been laissez-faire nor insensitive. The process of widening constitutional protection for the American press has been accompanied by the emergence of the Court as a primary arbiter and definer of its identity. The Court's characterizations of the press—as various as a fourth branch of government, a legitimate profession, and a wily Ulysses—together with the creation of extraordinary constitutional exemption from state control may well, in combination, have influenced the nature and development of the media.

Parallel to this is the evolution of the system of extensive public regulation of broadcast media. Its existence has meant not only that a significant portion of the American press has been regulated with an eye to maintaining and improving the level of public discussion but also that there has been a movement afoot with revolutionary potential for the media as a whole. Although the broadcast experiment has been isolated—by virtue of its official justification (that broadcasting is "unique"), by virtue of the language used in speaking about it (broadcasters are "trustees" not "editors"), and by virtue of the benign neglect exhibited by the First Amendment community (its omissions, e.g., from constitutional law casebooks)—there is good reason to suppose that the system has exerted profound, if subtle, effects on the character of the mass media in this country.

It is significant that, with regard to broadcast regulation, the Court has gone far beyond a posture of grudging toleration and has entertained a new way of conceiving of the relationship between the press, the public, and the state. Public control of private media power has been celebrated; in effect, tried on for size. It is significant that the rationale of broadcasting's uniqueness is so weak, in some forms intellectually indefensible and in another pointing to a phenomenon (concentration of power) increasingly characteristic of the media as a whole. And it is significant that the Court at times has written ambiguous opinions (as it did in *Red Lion*) about the potential relevance of the broadcast experiment for all media. These features of the broadcast regulation experience enhanced its relevance and hence its effect on the environment of the autonomy model of the print media, thus influencing the ways in which that freedom was actually utilized. The concepts underlying public regulation of broadcasting, as with the requirement of fairness in the presentation of viewpoints, have enunciated general norms of standard journalistic practice.

Viewed from another angle, the history of broadcast and cable regulation over the last half-century also suggests that the interaction of public regulation and constitutional adjudication has been used to instill and nurture standards of journalism in new communications technologies. By maintaining the notion that the autonomy model of the print media is at the core of the principle of freedom of the press, making print the norm and broadcasting the exception, a psychological atmosphere has been created, or reinforced, in which journalistic aspirations for new communications technologies are articulated.

Yet another thread composing the fabric of the American press, and one I have only lightly touched upon, is the creation of the system of public broadcasting. Any balanced evaluation of the experience of freedom of the press in this country cannot ignore the potential influence of that system on the press as a whole. Indeed, such an influence has been one of its explicit purposes. When public broadcasting was established in 1967, a primary motivation in its founding was its potential for reshaping public attitudes about the mass media not only in the arts but also in the discussion of public issues.[1] Public broadcasting would be an exemplar. Public broadcasting, therefore, is yet another key component in the complex use of law and public institutions to shape the character of the American press.

There is, then, a vast and as yet unfulfilled need to understand these potential reciprocal influences on the quality of discussion of public affairs within the American press. The analysis in this book has been largely at a conceptual level. Some data are available, but there is a clear need for much more. How, if at all, has the Court shaped the identity of the press? How, if at all, has public regulation of broadcasting shaped the print media? Has it been too powerful, making the media too homogeneous in character? To what extent do we want different identities, or journalistic styles, within the press? How much, if at all, have the print media and the Supreme Court been instrumental in inculcating journalistic values in new technologies? Is this a world in which protection follows only upon the emergence of a system of journalistic ethos? And what has been the role of public broadcasting? Before these questions can be answered, we also must begin to disaggregate the concerns about quality that are at stake.

To be sure, tracing and identifying these potential influences is a tremendously elusive task. It is also an imperative task. To undertake it, it would be wise to establish a modern sequel to the Hutchins commission. Much has changed in the quarter century since the commission's report, and today the most important matters calling for investigation are of a kind best suited to the perspective of a disinterested and independent commission.

I

Before we can be clearheaded in thinking about the great issues involving the press and the quality of public debate, however, it is critical that a new theoretical perspective be developed. Neither the organizing perspective of the autonomy model nor that of the public regulation model is adequate to the task at hand. Recall the 1985 FCC report and its claim that the fairness doctrine can and should be abandoned because the market has expanded sufficiently to remove the need for regulation. In its reasoning, the report is simply representative of a way of thinking about public regulation of media that needs to be examined. The commission reasoned as follows. The First Amendment embodies and reflects a basic value of this society, namely, that we share a commitment to seeking truth and wisdom, especially in matters of democratic decision making. We also share the belief that the best way to achieve this end is to have available a rich pool of information and ideas. With respect to broadcast media, however, physical limitations on the number of possible outlets has meant, at least in the past, that too few people will control this important means of access to the marketplace of ideas. Without correction through government regulation, the reasoning continues, we face an unhealthy situation in which broadcasters could manipulate public opinion, primarily by presenting biased programming. Hence, the fairness doctrine was devised to correct the market failure produced by the physical limitations of the electromagnetic spectrum.

Today, the commission continued, with the proliferation of broadcast outlets (cable, low-power television, etc.), as well as new forms emerging in the print media, the fear of extraordinary concentration that gave rise to the drastic remedy of government intervention is no longer reasonable.[2]

To this line of argument proponents of the fairness doctrine have generally responded in two ways. First, they argue that the supposed increase in availability of outlets has not yet been realized. Second, they claim that, even if the other media (notably print) are open and unconstricted, we should keep our eyes fixed only on the broadcast market, and on the opportunities for entry there, because broadcasting has a significantly greater "impact" on its audience than other media.[3] If true, they tell us, these facts compel us to regard broadcasting as a unique medium. In short, fairness doctrine proponents consider only the broadcasting and continue to point to the peculiar circumstances of market failure traditionally deemed characteristic of it.

These responses overlook a more central defect in the anti-fairness doctrine position. The problem arises from an assumed premise, the idea that the only acceptable rationale for public regulation must stem from some form of market failure. The commission's position seems to assume that people have no le-gitimate interest in public regulation as long as the total number of actual or potential outlets in the media is above a certain threshhold. In other words, as long as the shelf of information and ideas can be sufficiently stocked to satisfy consumer de-mand, there is no need for intervention. I think this is incorrect.

The first flaw in the commission's analysis is that it overlooks two major criticisms of a laissez-faire market system for the media. The first is that the market for freedom of the press necessarily exists within the larger context of a market for goods and services. This means that citizens arrive at the system of press freedom with vast inequalities of wealth and, therefore, with very different abilities to participate effectively in public debate.[4]

The second criticism is what Professor Owen Fiss has called the problem of "market reach," a term employed to distinguish it from other claims of market failure.[5] This refers to the conflict between the interests of those who manage for-profit media institutions and the interests of the democratic society in ensuring that citizens are supplied the information and ideas they ought to have: "[T]he market brings to bear on editorial and programming decisions factors that might have a great deal to do with profit-ability or allocative efficiency (to look at matters from a societal point of view) but little to do with the democratic needs of the electorate. . . . But there is no necessary, or even probabilistic, relationship between making a profit (or allocating resources efficiently) and supplying the electorate with the information they need to make free and intelligent choices about government policy, the structure of government, or the nature of society."[6]

But, as powerful as these additional criticisms are (additional to the criticism of excessive concentration of ownership), they do not provide as full and clear a picture as we need to determine the appropriate role of the state in mediating the deficiencies of a free press in the context of a free market system. They represent only an intermediate step toward a deeper, more fundamental understanding.

It is certainly true that, given the premises of the First Amendment, if only a few people or groups control access to the marketplace of ideas, then we have good reasons to be concerned about the power they wield. Those individuals may slight, or even omit, discussion of issues that deserve more attention, or they may skew the viewpoints presented about issues they do discuss. Either action can distort public discussion and decision making, producing unfortunate consequences for society.

Assuming that is true, it should immediately be apparent that the real concern is with power—that is, the ability to command an audience more or less exclusively—and that this concern is undiminished by the means by which such power is achieved. It makes no difference, in other words, whether power is the consequence of physical limitations associated with the use of the medium (the traditional assumption about broadcasting); or the result of limitations in the economic system (the traditional assumption about concentration of power in the daily newspaper market); or—and this is the generally unrecognized point—the result of market success in solidly appealing to a segment or majority of the community. The risks associated with power over access to the marketplace properly raise in us a sense of alarm; the source of that power does not. It is, therefore, a great mistake to assume that a large total number of entrants, or potential entrants, in the media, however defined, is by itself sufficient to quell that sense of alarm.

But now I want to shift the focus of concern in a new direction. To this point our attention has been directed primarily toward correcting the disparities of wealth underlying participation in the marketplace of ideas or toward defusing the power of those who happen to control the media. The question now is whether our thinking should move beyond the classical concerns of *New York Times v. Sullivan,* which stress the importance of remaining conscious of the risks of state intervention in the marketplace of ideas, a concern powerfully represented in the central image of how a regime of seditious libel can disable a democracy.

Unquestionably, we must be wary of the distortions caused by unequal distribution of wealth arising out of the general economic system. We must recognize also that those who happen to control mass media outlets will have their hearts in their pocketbooks, or in their own political agendas, not in the needs of citizens for full and fair information about public issues. But this does not fully capture the range of potential concerns, for we also must address the nature of our own behavior in the discussion of public questions—which means, in essense, to be concerned about the character of our demands in the market. We have good reason to be wary of ourselves, and we should fear not just the failures of the market system but our own failures of intellect. A democratic society, like an individual, should strive to remain conscious of the biases that skew, distort, and corrupt its own thinking about public issues. Society should be intellectually humble, in the way that a true education tries to inculcate respect for one's own ignorance and intellectual incapacities. The upshot is this: even in a world in which the press is entirely free and open to all voices, with a perfect market in that sense, human nature would still see to it that quality public debate and decision making would not rise naturally to the surface but would, in all probability, need the buoyant support of some form of collective action by citizens, involving public institutions.

Many of these potential biases, or failings of intellect, we have confronted already in the discussion thus far. Even in a world of unlimited opportunities we may not be sufficiently interested in informing ourselves about public issues, preferring entertainment and pleasure to the responsibilities of citizenship, a condition that recalls Brandeis's concern about the debilitating effects of invasions of privacy and gossip. We may not feel sufficiently educated to know what questions to ask about certain public issues or what level of deference to pay to expertise. We may fear that we do not understand what possible heights can be reached in art or in discussions of public issues. We may wish to avoid the opinions of those with whom we disagree, especially those on the margins of public debate, the radical voices. As a result, there may be a diaspora of viewpoints and an unheeding of troubled or troubling voices. We may not think clearly about some aspects of public issues. We may be too concerned with avoiding the costs of reasonable choices, too unwilling to accept an imperfect world (recall the *Pensions* case), or too unconcerned about the future costs of our choices and reforms, too willing to see greener grass in new alternatives (recall the *Banzhaf* case). We may have irrational prejudices against particular groups or individuals within society. Or we may be unduly influenced, and have our judgment distorted, by particular kinds of information in specific contexts.

These concerns exist independently of the amount of information available within the marketplace of ideas. They arise whether the shelf of ideas is full or not. They exist within each person, and may even be accentuated as the market becomes more uninhibited, robust, and wide open. And, in fact, these sorts of internal bias are not unknown, or unheeded, in this or any other liberal society. In our criminal justice system, for example, we go to great lengths to ensure the decision-making process is purified of biases, and we recognize that an entirely laissez-faire system is likely to produce great injustice. Our corrective efforts range from being attentive to the design and architecture of the space in which decisions are reached, in order to induce a solemn and deliberative atmosphere, to ensuring that certain kinds of evidence are admitted, and other kinds omitted, on the basis of their potential to prejudice the outcome. Society seems comfortable with these constraints within the criminal justice system, I suspect because we understand that the stakes are so high for the individual defendant.

The same is true of the way we think about democracy. The more democracy is realized, the higher the stakes, and the higher the stakes, the greater ought to be our concern with the problems of mental as well as market failure. It should be considered a sign of high intellectual development when a society is able to take steps to correct those problems within itself that interfere with quality decision making.

The concerns arise naturally out of today's mass media world. A few broadcasting networks reaching millions of people at the national level, and a single daily newspaper serving most residents in each local community, constitute the primary sources of information for the vast majority of citizens. That these national and local sources do not exhaust the potential for other entrants is clear; and that they give viewers and readers what they "want," or demand, through the expression of their preferences in the marketplace may be conceded. And yet it is hardly unimaginable that we—the same "we" that issue our marketplace votes for what we get—might be very concerned about how we are behaving, about what choices we are making, in that system. And we may, accordingly, decide together, through public regulation, that we would like to alter or modify the demands we find ourselves making in that market context.

This is the same thought that motivates groups or institutions to make decisions only in the context of a collective meeting. We recognize that if we are left to choose on our own whether and how to inform ourselves, too many will neglect to undertake the burdens of self-education, choosing instead to pursue more pleasant things. Or we may inform ourselves only selectively, following the natural inclination to seek out those with whom we agree.

Thus, even if we have the opportunity to acquire all relevant points of view, in the absence of agreed-upon structures or methods for deciding questions we may end up with poorer decisions. It is important, therefore, to recognize that public regulation requiring the media to grant access to the public under certain conditions need not be thought of as designed only to correct structural defects in the market. That too few people wield too much power over public discussion may be a sufficient justification for regulation, but it certainly is not a necessary condition for regulation. Other concerns may surface in its absence. We must, therefore, be careful not to make the mistake of thinking that public regulation hinges only on one possible rationale, and certainly not on the traditionally expressed rationale of market failure.

II

Thus it would be a more advanced society, a more advanced democratic society, that could act to correct deficiencies arising out of the structure of the marketplace of ideas but also arising out of the citizens themselves. That is not to say, however, that this society is, in fact, that advanced. The question is whether the society has reached a stage where the net gain of some reforms will be higher than that of staying put. To estimate the potential risks of reform will not be easy, but it will be fairly easy to know where to look for those risks. The real question is whether the government can be trusted with the power to intervene into the field of public debate.

This is not an issue that can be completely settled here, but there are several important points to consider. The first is an observation made by Professor Fiss, that we begin with the recognition that the government can never be excluded entirely from having a role in the marketplace of ideas, even in a strong laissez-faire system. That is because the government will be needed to do things such as, for example, use its police power to protect speakers against hecklers and disruption. This means not only that it would be quixotic to think of eliminating the government altogether but also that we do in fact have a body of experience with government intervention that may provide some relevant guidance on the question whether further intervention, intended to correct market and intellectual failures, is feasible.

The second point is simply another reminder that we do have specific relevant experience to guide us, namely, the regulation of broadcasting, cable television, and public broadcasting. It is, as I have argued before, imperative that this experience be studied closely. Until recently there has been a general consensus that the experience has been one of admirable self-restraint by the government, with few instances of abuse. But, as we saw in Chapter 6, that notion has begun to be challenged.

It is also important to bear in mind that, even if abuses have been minimal, the circumstances that produced restraint may not continue. It is possible that self-restraint has resulted from the special circumstances surrounding the partial regulatory system, especially the sense that any regulation was the exception to the general norm of a free press.

In the end, the question to be answered is whether the virtues of freedom of the press have become so internalized in our culture, by government and by the society at large, that society can afford to move, even if only very gradually, in the direction of new forms of self-correction. That will not be an easy question to answer, but it would be a pity if it were never asked or answered.

III

My purpose here has not been to assert that we should continue all the various kinds of controls on the quality of public discussion encountered throughout this book, nor that we should expand those controls or substitute others. My personal view is that most of the developments I have described seem, in general, to be healthy efforts. But I do not think I have made the full case for their continuance, in part because the information needed to make that case is lacking at the moment. My purpose, rather, has been to describe a system of exquisite complexity, one that has not been recognized as such, and to argue that the issues raised by this system demand our full and fair attention.

I do believe that our working conception of press freedom will change dramatically over the next century. The grand problem for the First Amendment and its principle of freedom of the press is that it is heading for, or may already have arrived at, a point at which a great intellectual transformation will occur. And, like all reformations, it will be neither simple nor bloodless. There are difficult and entrenched intellectual habits to overcome.

Although we are now in the process of leaving the age of innocence with respect to broadcast regulation, because the problematic character of the traditional rationales for regulation is manifest, the Supreme Court has given only the slightest hint that anything is amiss.[7] And this myopia is enhancing the growing movement for full First Amendment rights for cable television. The argument, first presented in 1971,[8] is that, since cable offers a multiplicity of channels, the scarcity rationale does not apply. That seems to make sense, and, as we have seen, that can go a long way in this area of the law. But it is not the number of channels that gives rise to the concern about "scarcity"; it is rather the number of *owners*. And, with cable there is only one owner, because cable is a natural monopoly (assuming one treats cable as a separate industry and does not see the exclusive franchise system as altering what would occur in a free market).[9]

There is a tendency in law—necessary but unfortunate—toward literalism. When it is said that "broadcasting can be regulated because the electromagnetic spectrum makes available only a limited number of channels," many people mistakenly assume that the statement draws significance from the fact that the spectrum is finite (the problem discussed in Chapter 6) and that the relevant concern is the number of channels. But the reference to the number of channels is simply a proxy for a deeper concern. The relevant fact is the number of people who control the channels. Unfortunately, with the advent of cable, by this literalism the traditional rationale for broadcasting is being hoisted, as it were, on its own pitard.

Furthermore, the central image of *New York Times v. Sullivan* contributes to an intellectual nearsightedness that is difficult to correct. To conceive of the government according to the image of seditious libel is to view it as inherently untrustworthy when it comes to public discussion. This, unfortunately, has the effect of driving a conceptual wedge between the citizens and the state, so that any regulation of the press is assumed to be democracy-depriving rather than potentially democracy-enhancing. Under this wilting perspective, all regulation loses its birthrights in the democratic process and becomes the apparent offspring of the authoritarian state. It will be criticized automatically as paternalistic and unworthy of a democracy, as emanating from an elitist distrust of the public mind.

But regulations such as public access rules, or systems of government subsidies like public broadcasting, need not be paternalistic in the classic sense. It is not paternalism when a majority of a society recognizes that its own intellectual limitations call for some institutional or structural correctives. When regulation stems from self-conscious awareness of biases, you do not have paternalism.[10] Regulation may be unwise for other reasons, but it need not be damned as stemming from an elitist vision.

It would be a great and important advance in the history of press freedom if there were a simple recognition that, *ideally,* the central image of the regime of seditious libel is one end of a spectrum that extends to another world in which quality discussion and decision making occur and public institutions are able to assist. This book has repeatedly stressed the vital importance to our thinking of the images we hold in our minds. We saw it in Kalven's praise for *New York Times v. Sullivan* as promising a method of reasoning about the First Amendment. We saw it in his speculation that we have become dull to the First Amendment implications of broadcast regulation because the Federal Communications Commission has never seriously abused its power. We saw it in Bickel's assertion that one of the costs of the *Pentagon Papers* case was that it gave us an image of government censorship that would forever make us feel less free. We saw it in the Hutchins commission report, as that body worried over the images of minority groups presented, or not presented, in the media. We saw it in cases like *Banzhaf* and *Pensions,* which dealt with the images of ourselves and of the world left us, as viewers, by advertisements and programs. We saw it in a traditional fear of the common law—the distorting power of facts— which the press itself knows as a potential defendant.

The images we live with have real power over us, including those provided by the courts. It is, therefore, crucial that courts begin to develop a more realistic set of images than that incorporating a regime of seditious libel.

The most powerful force driving us toward that more complex vision, even more powerful than the increasing visibility of the broadcast regulation experiment, is likely to come from an unexpected quarter. It is the emerging so-called right to gather the news. On the newsgathering side, we are being forced to confront the disconcerting fact that much information in this or any society is better left unspoken, often because of a legitimate distrust of the process of public discussion. As this occurs, we will come to discover that the law of property is relied upon to protect us from completely "uninhibited" and "wide-open" dissemination of information, while we claim a contrary self-image.

IV

In earlier chapters it was noted that the Supreme Court has applied the newsgathering right only in the context of criminal trials. During the 1970s, three cases came before the Court in which the press sought a First Amendment right of access to prisons. The press lost in each case.[11] Initially, the press even failed in its efforts to obtain access to trials.[12] *Richmond Newspapers*, in 1980, finally broke the newsgathering right barrier.[13] The earlier cases, however, remain significant because they indicate that the Court will face continual pressures to venture outside the realm of the criminal trial, or perhaps the judicial system, with the newsgathering right.

One dilemma that this right poses is that it puts courts squarely in the middle of a vast uncharted terrain, where it must face the need for limitations on the general value of "uninhibited, robust, and wide-open" debate. The importance of confidentiality, of privacy, even of secrecy, in government affairs is tremendous. The press should be acutely aware of this fact, given its own assertion in *Branzburg* of the need for respecting the secrecy of its sources. And the Court itself is acutely aware of this fact, too, since it always takes care to indicate that some areas of government affairs—its own conferences, for example—will be forever outside the boundaries of the newsgathering right.[14] But there is, of course, also a tremendous value in openness. The public must know what is happening within official quarters, not only to maintain the ability to participate effectively but also for the purifying effect public scrutiny has on the decision-making process—giving rise to the metaphor that sunshine is the best disinfectant. A compelling logic in the newsgathering right says that the right to speak is meaningless if one has nothing to report.

All this points to the massiveness of the enterprise of developing a general newsgathering right, which is in itself a problem. If the Court tries to consider cases outside the area of judicial proceedings, it may be overwhelmed by the burden of deciding literally thousands of cases in which the press claims a right of access to this or that body of information or to this or that proceeding so that it can perform its role of reporting on the day's events to the public at large.

A second, and not inconsiderable, question is whether, assuming that the courts are prepared to handle this burden of cases, judges are capable of weighing the competing interests at stake and of understanding the importance of the government interest involved. One might, of course, object that the Court already weighs competing interests when it considers government efforts to curtail freedom of speech and press. In *Pentagon Papers,* for example, it weighed and evaluated the government's claim that publication of the voluminous documents would seriously threaten national security interests of the country against the First Amendment interest in open and full debate. In the end, as we know, the Court found the government's claim wanting. The question might be asked, Isn't the newsgathering right only asking the Court to do what it already does?

The answer, I think, is yes, but there is still a difference that needs to be considered. We have managed, so far without doing serious damage to society, to live with a system in which constitutional protection for speaking and publishing is extraordinary, in some cases very nearly absolute, and includes the freedom to communicate information that can cause great harm. But it may well be that the only reason the right to speak and publish can be so broad is that the system of property rights is also broad. If the press knew or had access to every fact about our lives, the constitutional value of the right to sue for publication of highly embarrassing facts would skyrocket.

The key thought, then, is this: that we are comfortable with taking freedom of speech and press to the lengths we do, and permitting judges to decide when the costs are too great, only because we know in our hearts that truly harmful situations will rarely arise because we retain the ability to keep really dangerous information secret. There is evidence for this in the *Progressive* case, in which (it will be recalled) the government attempted to halt publication of an article on how to make a hydrogen bomb. When the government filed its suit in federal district court, it submitted affidavits from high government officials and distinguished scientists describing the harm that could arise from publication. It claimed, among other things, that within seven years terrorists would have the capability of producing a hydrogen bomb. The district court judge was so obviously moved by this startling assertion that he issued the first injunction ever against the press on national security grounds.[15] Although the claim apparently was specious, its plausibility in the free speech context makes one appreciate the fact that freedom of speech and press covers only a part, perhaps even a small part, of the world's store of information.

Alexander Bickel, one of our most distinguished constitutional scholars, represented the New York Times in the *Pentagon Papers* case and afterward wrote that it will never be feasible to develop a press (or public) right to obtain government-held information. He proposed instead to maintain the "untidy" world that existed at the time of *Pentagon Papers,* in which the government was free to do all it could, using the system of property rights, to stop the press from getting information; and the press, on its side, could publish just about anything it could get its hands on. Such a system posed the potentially serious costs of keeping too much information from the public, of making hollow freedom of speech and press, and of allowing very harmful information to be published with impunity. This, Bickel thought, was better than a more orderly system of judicial intervention that would compel some disclosure but also possibly cut back on the freedom to publish.[16]

It is, of course, impossible to say how far the *Richmond Newspapers* newsgathering right will be extended. Perhaps it will not extend beyond judicial proceedings, where the Court obviously felt comfortable making its first tentative move, no doubt because it feels it understands the risks involved. If not, then the case will be a prime candidate for illustrating that distinguished social function of freedom of speech and press, discussed in Chapter 3, of serving as a kind of symbolic projectile of an underrepresented value (here the value of openness) launched into the general social fray. Then, too, the Court could continue to use the distorted and oversimplified images that are the luxury of symbolism. But I doubt that either will happen. The newsgathering right is young and just gathering muscle. As the right expands so, too, will, by necessity, the sensitivity and depth of analysis. Consider, as a metaphor, a case from the state of New Jersey, *State v. Lashinsky.*[17]

Lashinsky, a news photographer, was driving along a freeway when he observed a car that had crashed through the barrier. He stopped and found inside a decapitated woman and her daughter, still alive but pinned in the car and going into shock. Lashinsky took photographs. Others stopped until there was a crowd of forty to fifty people. A state trooper arrived who, seeing large amounts of cash strewn around, leaking gasoline, and a cracked battery, ordered the crowd to move up a hill. Lashinsky refused. For some time, and while a medical aide tried to minister to the dying woman and sought the assistance of the officer, the trooper and Lashinsky engaged in a heated argument. Lashinsky claimed that he was a member of the press (showing his press pass) and should be permitted to remain at the site and take pictures; the officer insisted that he move back with the crowd. After repeated refusals to leave, Lashinsky was arrested by the officer. Lashinsky was convicted under a statute prohibiting persons from disobeying the reasonable order of a police officer. Lashinsky claimed, among other things, a First Amendment right to be present at the scene of an accident.

As grotesque and seemingly bizarre as the *Lashinsky* case is, it is representative of the kinds of free press issues we can expect to confront in the future. How is one to think about a problem like this? Platitudes such as "the press is the representative of the public," "the public has a right to know," "the government cannot be trusted," "sunshine is the best disinfectant," and "debate on public issues should be uninhibited, robust, and wide-open" will no longer have quite the ring of decisive helpfulness that they seem to in other contexts. The issue of how to advance the social and First Amendment interest in quality public decision making is difficult and deeply troubling.

Should one weigh the value of this kind of "information," and, if so, by what standards? Why is it important to have photographs of decapitated bodies and victims of car accidents? Putting aside the sensitivities of the individuals and their relations, is this pandering to baser instincts in people unworthy of First Amendment protection? On the other hand, is this the kind of visual information that can be used so effectively to help us think more clearly about issues such as car safety requirements, seat-belt laws, and highway regulations? More difficult yet is the problem of judging where our interest in quality decision making within a democracy leads on the matter of sunshine or secrecy. Just as in a trial, the ability of the press to observe public officials performing their duties is a powerful check against poor performance. The officer and the medic might perform better with the press standing right there. On the other hand, they might do worse. In this case, being observed may bring pressures that will produce a poorer performance overall. No one, including Supreme Court justices in their conferences, fully trusts the public to put issues in their proper perspective or digest information fairly. And having the press present may create opportunities for unproductive conflict—and the public lies dying while both the public officials and the press avoid their distressing duties by engaging in heated argument with each other.

The aim here is not to answer the specific issue of *Lashinsky*[18] but to make a larger and more general point. That point begins with the observation that there is no "principle" by which one can decide when secrecy or openness will produce the best decision making.[19] Such a decision will always depend upon one's understanding and analysis of the character and social context of the relevant participants. Sometimes secrecy is a cloak for bad motives or behavior; sometimes it is a necessary condition for the exercise of fair and good judgment. The development and extension of this kind of First Amendment psychology, which Harry Kalven sensed with pleasure emerging from the Court's analysis in *New York Times v. Sullivan,* will be important in its own right. And in doing that it will be necessary to face the truth—which thus far the *Sullivan* analysis of freedom of speech and press ignores—that there are definite and substantial limits on our willingness to trust the process of wide-open public debate with all information.

V

Freedom of the press, then, is approaching a turning point. Part of the problem will be simply deciding which way to turn. A major question is whether public regulation of the electronic media should be continued or even extended. Serious issues dealing with the scope of legal actions for invasion of privacy and the newsgathering right will have to be faced. But in large measure this upheaval will be conceptual, driven primarily by a breakdown in the rhetoric of broadcast regulation and by the recognition of a newsgathering right. Developments such as those now occurring in the libel area, with the analysis of requirements such as "public controversies," newsworthiness, and the fact-opinion distinction will also make a contribution. But, like the two cutting edges of very large shears, the vastly different First Amendment analyses for the print media and for the electronic media, together with the very different analyses for restrictions on speech and for restrictions on access to information, are gradually coming together. And as they do they should bring into being a more integrated and complex analysis of the idea of freedom of the press, one that already has roots in places like the fairness doctrine—and the central image of *New York Times v. Sullivan* will be displaced.

POSTSCRIPT

The idea of press autonomy, so dominant in our notions about the American principle of freedom of the press, has its moderating, its shaping, influences. The extraordinary experiment with public regulation of new communications technologies in this century is one. Another is the images about journalism and public debate emanating from the ever-growing jurisprudence of mass media law, composed of a mixture of constitutional, statutory, and common law. Viewed as a whole, we are confronted with a deeply complex, interdependent, blended system—a system with its own ecology.

The particular forms of public regulation of the electronic media must be fairly evaluated. But the rationality of that regulatory scheme, involving the differential treatment of the electronic and print media, also must be understood anew. Up to now the system has thrived on an intellectual posture in which the fundamental premises of each branch are treated as utterly discrete and largely self-evident. That has had the benefits of permitting the full exploration of a lived reality and of avoiding slipping down the slope of regulatory abuse. It has, however, also come with serious costs. One cost is that the general relevance of ideas entertained in the context of the electronic media—such as the concern over the potential for adverse impact of media on the minds of the audience—have at times been stunted. Another is that the implicit assumption about the need to locate a material difference to justify a system of differential treatment is now causing the fictions employed to outdo good sense, as public policy in this area is being reconsidered. And, finally, it is unfortunate, and ironic, that the system has operated by taking advantage of an intellectual tendency—to disregard the costs of choices—that is simultaneously a matter of concern (in cases like *Pensions*) in thinking about the character of public debate. It would be preferable, all things considered, if the system operated with greater self-knowledge.

The relationship between the growing jurisprudence of mass media law, including its accompanying images of the press, and the character of public debate in the media also requires further study. The analyses now occurring in areas such as libel, invasion of privacy, newsgathering, and the fairness doctrine all converge to produce an expanding set of working assumptions about the character of the press and public debate, far beyond what Harry Kalven speculated would occur after *New York Times v. Sullivan*. To ask, as the public figure doctrine in libel, the newsworthiness doctrine in privacy, and the fairness doctrine all do, whether a given discussion is about a valuable issue or public controversy is to define a hierarchy of public discussions. To ask why privacy interests decline and the interests of public debate increase when a private fact is revealed to expose the hypocrisy of a speaker is to understand the importance of sincerity in public discourse. To ask whether one side of a controversial issue of public importance has been presented, or to ask whether a given statement would be taken by the average reader as implying certain facts and be believed, is to explore the nature of (what the Hutchins commission called) the public mentality. And to ask whether information should be accessible or not to the press and to the public, as the newsgathering right does, is to define the nature and degree of democracy itself.

These and other inquiries undertaken over time, along with the other images developed through the process, will interact with the development of the identity of the press, in the way that the evolution of a system of commercial law over the centuries has interacted with commercial practices. That interaction will take place not only at the grand level of Supreme Court pronouncements but also at the grass roots level of the attorney in the editorial room. Lawyers and editors spend more time together today than ever before, in discussions (I am regularly told) that go beyond points of law. That newer relationship between "law" and journalism must be better understood than it is now. But, more than anything, it is important not to lose sight of the larger and more fundamental insight that the underlying foundations of this emerging system of law will have effects beyond those of any particular doctrine or set of doctrines.

CHAPTER ONE

1. 376 U.S. 254 (1964).

2. Id. at 257–58.

3. Kalven, "The New York Times Case: A Note on 'The Central Meaning of the First Amendment,'" 1964 Sup. Ct. Rev. 191, 195–96.

4. 376 U.S. at 278 n. 18.

5. *Chaplinsky v. New Hampshire*, 315 U.S. 568, 572 (1942).

6. 376 U.S. at 275 (quoting Madison, 4 Annals of Cong. 934 [1794].

7. The Sedition Act provided: "That if any person shall write, print, utter or publish, or shall cause or procure to be written, printed, uttered or published, or shall knowingly and willingly assist or aid in writing, printing, uttering or publishing any false, scandalous and malicious writing or writings against the government of the United States, or either house of the Congress of the United States, or the President of the United States, with intent to defame the said government, or either house of the said Congress, or the said President, or to bring them, or either of them, into contempt or disrepute; or to excite against them, or either or any of them, the hatred of the good people of the United States, or to stir up sedition within the United States, or to excite any unlawful combinations therein, for opposing or resisting any law of the United States, or any act of the President of the United States, done in pursuance of any such law, or of the powers in him vested by the constitution of the United States, or to resist, oppose, or defeat any such law or act, or to aid, encourage or abet any hostile designs of any foreign nation against the United States, their people or government, then such person, being thereof convicted before any

court of the United States having jurisdiction thereof, shall be punished by a fine not exceeding two thousand dollars, and by imprisonment not exceeding two years." Sedition Act, ch. 73, sec. 2, 1 Stat. 596, 596–97 (1798), *repealed by* Sedition Act, ch. 73, sec. 4, 1 Stat. 596, 597 (1801).

8. 376 U.S. at 273.

9. Id. at 279 n.19 (quoting Mill, *On Liberty* [Oxford: Blackwell, 1947], 15).

10. Id. at 271 (quoting *Cantwell v. Connecticut,* 310 U.S. 296, 310 [1940]).

11. "[T]o argue sophistically, to suppress facts or arguments, to misstate the elements of the case, or misrepresent the opposite opinion . . . all this, even to the most aggravated degree, is so continually done in perfect good faith, by persons who are not considered, and in many other respects may not deserve to be considered, ignorant or incompetent, that it is rarely possible, on adequate grounds, conscientiously to stamp the misrepresentation as morally culpable; and still less could law presume to interfere with this kind of controversial misconduct." 376 U.S. at 272 n.13 (quoting Mill, *On Liberty* [Oxford: Blackwell, 1947], 47).

12. Id. at 270.

13. Kalven, "The New York Times Case," at 212–13.

14. Id. at 221.

15. *Rosenbloom v. Metromedia, Inc.,* 403 U.S. 29 (1971) (plurality opinion). Justice Brennan, joined by Chief Justice Burger and Justice Blackmun, announced the judgment of the Court that the constitutional standard of knowing or reckless falsity applied whenever the allegedly defamatory statements related to the plaintiff's involvement in a matter of public concern. Justice Black concurred on the ground that the First Amendment did not permit recovery of libel judgments against the news media, even when the media acted with knowledge that the statements were false. Justice White also concurred, expressing the view that, lacking the requisite showing of knowledge or reckless falsity under the constitutional standard, the press had a privilege under the First Amendment to report and comment on official actions of public servants. Justice Harlan dissented, stating that, although fault must be demonstrated in defamation cases, the states should be free to impose a duty of reasonable care in defamation cases involving a private plaintiff, and the plaintiff should be compensated only for actual harm that was

reasonably foreseeable as a result of the publication. Justice Marshall, joined by Justice Stewart, dissented on the grounds that states should be free to establish whatever fault standard best suited the state's needs as long as a strict liability standard was not employed and damages were restricted to actual losses.

16. *Gertz v. Robert Welch, Inc.,* 418 U.S. 323 (1974).

17. Id. at 345.

18. Id.

19. 424 U.S. 448 (1976).

20. Id. at 454.

21. 443 U.S. 157 (1979).

22. 443 U.S. 111 (1979).

23. Id. at 115.

24. See *Dun & Bradstreet, Inc. v. Greenmoss Builders, Inc.,* 472 U.S. 749 (1985).

25. 418 U.S. at 347.

26. See *Philadelphia Newspapers, Inc. v. Hepps,* 475 U.S. 767, 768 (1986).

27. 472 U.S. at 758.

28. 418 U.S. at 350.

29. See *Milkovich v. Lorain Journal Co.,* 497 U.S.—, 110 Sup. Ct. 2695 (1990).

30. *New York Times Co. v. United States* [Pentagon Papers Case], 403 U.S. 713 (1971).

31. Id. at 763 (Justice Blackmun dissenting) (quoting *United States v. Washington Post Co.,* 446 F.2d 1327, 1330 [1971]).

32. Id. at 714 (per curiam).

33. Id.

34. 418 U.S. 241 (1974).

35. Id. at 256.

36. Id. at 258.

37. Id.

38. 420 U.S. 469 (1975).

39. Id. at 487.

40. Id. at 491.

41. Id. at 491–92.

42. Id. at 496.

43. Id.

44. 491 U.S.—; 109 Sup. Ct. 2603 (1989).

45. Id. at 2607.

46. Id. at 2609.

47. Id.

48. Id. at 2611.

49. 485 U.S. 46 (1988).

50. Id. at 48.

51. 460 U.S. 575 (1983).

52. Id. at 585.

53. 481 U.S. 221 (1987).

54. 427 U.S. 539 (1976).

55. Id. at 568–69.

56. 448 U.S. 555 (1980).

57. In *Richmond Newspapers, Inc. v. Virginia,* the Court stated: "[T]he historical evidence demonstrates conclusively that at the time when our organic laws were adopted, criminal trials both here and in England had long been presumptively open. This is no quirk of history; rather, it has long been recognized as an indispensable attribute of an Anglo-American trial. Both Hale in the 17th century and Blackstone in the 18th saw the importance of openness to the proper functioning of a trial; it gave assurance that the proceedings were conducted fairly to all concerned, and it discouraged perjury, the misconduct of participants, and decisions based on secret bias or partiality." 448 U.S. at 555, 569. The Court further stated: "The early history of open trials in part reflects the widespread acknowledgment, long before there were behavioral scientists, that public trials had significant community therapeutic value. Even without such experts to frame the concept in words, people sensed from experience and observation that, especially in the administration of criminal justice, the means used to achieve justice must have the support derived from public acceptance of both the process and its results." Id. at 570–71.

58. Id. at 587 (Justice Brennan concurring).

59. 457 U.S. 596 (1982).

60. 464 U.S. 501 (1984).

61. 478 U.S. 1 (1986).

62. Id. at 14.

63. 408 U.S. 665 (1972).

64. Id. at 680.

65. Id. at 692.

66. 436 U.S. 547 (1978).

67. The Court summarized the press's argument: "The general submission is that searches of newspaper offices for evidence of crime reasonably believed to be on the premises will seriously threaten the ability of the press to gather, analyze, and disseminate news. This is said to be true for several reasons: First, searches will be physically disruptive to such an extent that timely publication will be impeded. Second, confidential sources of information will dry up, and the press will also lose opportunities to cover various events because of fears of the participants that press files will be readily available to the authorities. Third, reporters will be deterred from recording and preserving their recollections for future use if such information is subject to seizure. Fourth, the processing of news and its dissemination will be chilled by the prospects that searches will disclose internal editorial deliberations. Fifth, the press will resort to self-censorship to conceal its possession of information of potential interest to the police." Id. at 563–64.

68. Id. at 566.

69. Id. at 570 (Justice Powell concurring). In *Branzburg,* Justice Powell wrote to "emphasize" the "limited nature of the Court's holding," and he observed that, given the Court's "solicitude" for the First Amendment, any journalist who "believes that the grand jury investigation is not being conducted in good faith" is "not without remedy." He continued, "Indeed, if the newsman is called upon to give information bearing only a remote and tenuous relationship to the subject of the investigation, or if he has some other reason to believe that his testimony implicates confidential source relationships without a legitimate need of law enforcement, he will have access to the court on a motion to quash and an appropriate protective order may be entered." *Branzburg v. Hayes,* 408 U.S. 665, 709–10 (Justice Powell concurring).

70. For literature debating the special role of the press in the political system and the issue of special First Amendment rights for

the press, see, e.g., Stewart, "Or of the Press," 26 Hastings L. J. 631 (1975); Blasi, "The Checking Value in First Amendment Theory," 1977 Am. Bar Found. Res. J. 521; Lange, "The Speech and Press Clauses," 23 UCLA L. Rev. 77 (1975); Lewis, "A Preferred Position for Journalism?" 7 Hof. L. Rev. 595 (1979); Van Alstyne, "The Hazards to the Press of Claiming a 'Preferred Position,'" 28 Hast. L. J. 761 (1977); Abrams, "The Press Is Different: Reflections on Justice Stewart and the Autonomous Press," 7 Hof. L. Rev. 563 (1979); Bollinger, "The Press and the Public Interest: An Essay on the Relationship between Social Behavior and the Language of First Amendment Theory," 82 Mich. L. Rev. 1447 (1984).

71. For the argument that the principal First Amendment value of the press is its capacity to detect and reveal government abuse of power, and not its ability to facilitate an active democratic exchange among citizens, see Blasi, "The Checking Value in First Amendment Theory," at 521.

CHAPTER TWO

1. The total number of daily newspapers in the United States declined from 2,042 in 1920 to 1,745 in 1988. U.S. Bureau of the Census, *Historical Statistics of the United States: Colonial Times to 1970,* bicentennial ed. (Washington, D.C., 1989), 809; U.S. Bureau of the Census, *Statistical Abstract of the United States: 1989,* 109th ed. (Washington, D.C., 1989), 549.

2. Statistics are difficult to come by on this matter, but a safe estimate would be that approximately 20 cities have independently owned competing daily newspapers. See Sanders, "Aftermath of the Death of the St. Louis Globe-Democrat: Are Failing Newspapers Still Worth Preserving?" 33 St. Louis Univ. L. J. 1005, 1015–16 (1989).

3. Commission on Freedom of the Press, *A Free and Responsible Press* (Chicago: University of Chicago Press, 1947).

4. Id. at v–vi.

5. Id. at vi. In addition to the summary report, the individual members of the commission produced six other books, all published by the University of Chicago Press: *Government and Mass Communications* by Zechariah Chafee, Jr.; *Freedom of the Press: A Framework of Principle* by William Ernest Hocking; *Freedom of the Movies: A Report on Self-Regulation* by Ruth A. Inglis; *The American Press and the San Francisco Conference* by Milton D. Stewart; *Peoples*

Speaking to Peoples: A Report on International Mass Communication by Llewellyn White and Robert D. Leigh; and *The American Radio* by Llewellyn White.

6. Commission on Freedom of the Press, *A Free and Responsible Press,* at 1.

7. Id. at 68.

8. Id. at 96–97.

9. Id.

10. Id. at 14.

11. Id.

12. Id. at 15.

13. Id. at 43.

14. Id. at 48.

15. Id. at 20–21.

16. Id. at 23.

17. Id. at 25.

18. Id. at 26.

19. Id. at 52.

20. Id.

21. Id. at 68.

22. Id. at 52–53.

23. Id. at 53.

24. Id. at 55.

25. Id. at 55–56.

26. Id. at 65.

27. Id. at 12.

28. Id. at 8–10.

29. Id. at 19, 80.

30. Id. at 92.

31. Id.

32. A recent biography of Hutchins describes how the commission report was received by the press:

The reaction to publication of the report by what was promptly dubbed the Hutchins Commission demonstrated the validity of one of its key findings—that the press consistently suppressed or distorted criticism of its own performance. "No other institution could have been criticized by so distinguished a group as Chancellor Hutchins' commission without having its indictment land on the front page," observed Louis M. Lyons, curator of Harvard's Nieman Foundation. The most complete report, three and a half columns in the *New York Times,* was buried on page 24. Many newspapers, including those of the Hearst chain, ignored it altogether. Others topped brief extracts from wire-service coverage with misleading headlines.

A few newspapers provided approving editorial comment, generally echoing Walter Lippmann, who endorsed the proposal for continuing outside criticism by citing the traditional claim that the Fourth Estate was the watchdog of the other three, and inquiring, "Who watches the watchman, who inspects the inspector, who polices the policeman?" The great bulk of newspaper and magazine comment was adverse, at its mildest dismissing the Commission's findings as the work of airy-fairy college professors who ignored the reality of the communications marketplace. A few editorial writers thought they detected subversion, and the *Wall Street Journal* even caught a whiff of Communism.

The report, as *Newsweek* noted, raised every one of Colonel Robert R. McCormick's hackles. The *Chicago Tribune's* opening blast appeared under the headline "A FREE PRESS (HITLER STYLE) SOUGHT FOR U.S.; TOTALITARIANS TELL HOW IT CAN BE DONE." Frank Hughes, a hatchet man regularly assigned to traducing the University, was given paid leaves of absence to crank out a book, *Prejudice and the Press: A Restatement of the Principle of Freedom of the Press with Specific Reference to the Hutchins-Luce Commission.*

"If there is a disposition in some important quarters of American opinion today to question freedom of the press, to seek to 're-define' it, and to make it more 'accountable,' these efforts can come only from the apostles of despotism," Hughes declared in the opening chapter of his 640-page work. In inimitable *Tribune* style he went on to explain why this was so:

The philosophy to which Chancellor Hutchins pretends, containing . . . the basic authoritarianism of the Prussians, with a dash of Plato, and much Aristotle and Aquinas interpreted by Adler, according to Marx, is a curious mixture. . . . It cannot be labeled definitely as Communist or as Nazi, although it contains elements of both.

Couched in less extreme terms, the charge that the Commission advocated an unwarranted and dangerous abrogation of First Amendment rights was echoed by more responsible publications—this despite the fact that the report specifically opposed any form of government intervention. This fallacious notion became imbedded in the mythology that surrounded Hutchins' public image, and his response to it over the years was a major item in what he called his antiabsurdity campaign. (Harry S. Ashmore, *Unseasonable Truths: The Life of Robert Maynard Hutchins* [Boston: Little, Brown & Co., 1989], 296–97).

33. See, e.g., *A Free and Responsive Press: 20th Century Task Force Report for a National News Council* (New York: Twentieth Century Fund, 1972); B. Bagdikian, *The Media Monopoly*, 3rd ed. (Boston: Beacon Press, 1990). For a similar analysis of mass communications in Great Britain, see R. Williams, *Communications*, 3d ed. (New York: Penguin, 1976).

34. See, e.g., Reisman, "Democracy and Defamation: Control of Group Libel," 42 Colum. L. Rev. 727 (1942).

35. For a current summary of the literature, see Schudson, "The Sociology of News Production," in *Media, Culture and Society*, vol. 11 (London: Sage, 1989), 263–82.

36. See, e.g., Wellington, "On Freedom of Expression," 88 Yale L. J. 1105, 1114 (1979), quoted in Bollinger, *The Tolerant Society* (New York: Oxford University Press, 1986), 223–24: "The candidate, to the contrary, begs the court to recognize that the lies published about him misled the voters and thereby injured the political process. The statutory standard of due care, he insists, is the ideal standard for ensuring that the public is informed, rather than misled. Negligence is not to be encouraged in the reporting of political news any more than elsewhere, and if due care costs more than carelessness, the purpose of the First Amendment requires that newspapers rather than voters should bear that cost. Moreover, if newspapers are free to lie, some of our most capable citizens will be

deterred from running for office; the risk to reputation may outweigh the charm of the public life."

37. Warren and Brandeis, "The Right to Privacy," 4 Harv. L. Rev. 193 (1890).

38. Id. at 196.

39. "It is urged that at the time the First Amendment to the Constitution was enacted in 1791 as part of our Bill of Rights the press was broadly representative of the people it was serving. While many of the newspapers were intensely partisan and narrow in their views, the press collectively presented a broad range of opinions to readers. . . . A true marketplace of ideas existed in which there was relatively easy access to the channels of communication. Access advocates submit that although newspapers of the present are superficially similar to those of 1791 the press of today is in reality very different from that known in the early years of our national existence. . . . Newspapers have become big business and there are far fewer of them to serve a larger literate population. Chains of newspapers, national newspapers, national wire and news services, and one-newspaper towns are the dominant features of a press that has become noncompetitive and enormously powerful and influential in its capacity to manipulate popular opinion and change the course of events. . . . The elimination of competing newspapers in most of our large cities, and the concentration of control of media that results from the only newspaper's being owned by the same interests which own a television station and a radio station, are important components of this trend toward concentration of control of outlets to inform the public. The result of these vast changes has been to place in a few hands the power to inform the American people and shape public opinion. Much of the editorial opinion and commentary that is printed is that of syndicated columnists distributed nationwide and, as a result, we are told, on national and world issues there tends to be a homogeneity of editorial opinion, commentary and interpretive analysis. The abuses of bias and manipulative reportage are, likewise, said to be the result of the vast accumulations of unreviewable power in the modern media empires. In effect, it is claimed, the public has lost any ability to respond or to contribute in a meaningful way to the debate on issues. The monopoly of the means of communication allows for little or no critical analysis of the media except in professional journals of very limited readership." *Miami Herald Publishing Co. v. Tornillo*, 418 U.S. at 241, 248–50.

40. The National News Council was established in 1973. At that time, Arthur Ochs Sulzberger, publisher of the New York Times, expressed the fear that the council would divert attention from the actions of government officials which, he felt, were the real threat. Jonathan Friendly, "National News Council Will Dissolve," New York Times, 23 March 1984, Late City Final edition, sec. B, p. 18, col. 1. When the council suspended operations in 1984, Richard S. Salant, its president, claimed that "fear of unwarranted intrusion seemed to be the major obstacle to the Council's effort to win the support it needed from the media." "National News Council Folds," United Press International, 23 March 1984, PM cycle, Domestic News section. News executives, whose organizations occasionally boycotted the council, "question whether any organization can oversee the complicated, diverse American press, and note that such councils rarely have adequate research help." William A. Henry III, "Journalism under Fire," Time, 12 December 1983, at 91.

CHAPTER THREE

1. "The judgments of the Court ought . . . to instruct and to inspire." "Address by William J. Brennan, Jr.," 32 Rutg. L. Rev. 173, 174 (1979).

2. Bob Woodward and Scott Armstrong, *The Brethren: Inside the Supreme Court* (New York: Simon and Schuster, 1979).

3. For example, in *Hustler Magazine, Inc. v. Falwell*, 485 U.S. 46 (1988), Falwell argued that a parody portraying him as having engaged in a drunken incestuous rendezvous with his mother in an outhouse was so "outrageous" that it could not be compared with "traditional political cartoons." The Court responded: "There is no doubt that the caricature of respondent and his mother published in Hustler is at best a distant cousin of the political cartoons described above, and a rather poor relation at that. If it were possible by laying down a principled standard to separate one from the other, public discourse would probably suffer little or no harm. But we doubt that there is any such standard, and we are quite sure that the pejorative description 'outrageous' does not supply one." 485 U.S. at 55.

For a sophisticated analysis of the developing concept of "public discourse," see Post, "The Constitutional Concept of Public Discourse: Outrageous Opinion, Democratic Deliberation, and *Hustler Magazine v. Falwell*," 103 Harv. L. Rev. 601 (1990).

4. See, e.g., *Kassel v. Gannett Co., Inc.*, 875 F.2d 935, 944 (1st Cir. 1989) (newspaper's negligence was shown by its failure to verify a story where time was not a critical problem and the means of verification were readily at hand); *Stone v. Banner Publishing Corp.*, 677 F. Supp. 242, 247 (D. Vt. 1988) (newspaper was negligent in relying on a police investigator's report and statements without investigating further); *Jones v. Palmer Communications, Inc.*, 440 N.W.2d 884, 898 (Iowa 1989) (court applied a professional standard of care, which is the degree of care ordinarily prudent persons in the press usually exercise in similar conditions); *Rouch v. Enquirer & News of Battle Creek*, 427 Mich. 157, 398 N.W.2d 245, 259 (1986) (court surveyed states that had adopted the negligence standard as a matter of state defamation law).

5. See *Rosenbloom v. Metromedia, Inc.*, 403 U.S. 29 (1971).

6. *Gertz v. Robert Welch, Inc.*, 418 U.S. 323, 346 (1974).

7. Id. at 345.

8. See *Time v. Firestone*, 424 U.S. 448 (1976). The Court stated: "Dissolution of a marriage through judicial proceedings is not the sort of 'public controversy' referred to in *Gertz*, even though the marital difficulties of extremely wealthy individuals may be of interest to some portion of the reading public. Nor did respondent freely choose to publicize issues as to the propriety of her married life. She was compelled to go to court by the State in order to obtain legal release from the bonds of matrimony." Id. at 454.

In a footnote, the Court argued that, although Mrs. Firestone held press conferences "to satisfy inquiring reporters," this did not convert her into a "public figure." Id. at 454, n.3. The Court reasoned that these press conferences had no effect on the merits of the divorce proceeding nor was there any intention to affect the proceeding. Id. Moreover, the Court found no indication that Mrs. Firestone "sought to use the press conferences as a vehicle by which to thrust herself to the forefront of some unrelated controversy in order to influence its resolution." Id.

While the Court treated the Firestone divorce trial as the only "controversy," it had other options. For example, it viewed the controversy as preexisting the divorce trial and involving the stormy marriage of wealthy Palm Beach socialites.

9. Justice Marshall, dissenting in *Firestone*, warned that the Court, under the guise of defining "public controversy," was making judgments about what kind of speech to protect. To the ma-

jority, Marshall said that "[t]he controversy was not of the sort deemed relevant to the 'affairs of society' and the public's interest not of the sort deemed 'legitimate' or worthy of judicial recognition." 448 U.S. at 487.

Marshall found that the Court's case-by-case judgment of what kind of speech is worthy of protection was in direct contradiction to *Gertz*. "If *Gertz* is to have any meaning at all the focus of analysis must be on the actions of the individual, and the degree of public attention that had already developed, or that could have been anticipated, before the report in question." Id. at 489.

10. See *Restatement of Torts, Second* (1965), sec. 652D: Publicity Given to Private Life: "One who gives publicity to a matter concerning the private life of another is subject to liability to the other for invasion of his privacy, if the matter publicized is of a kind that (a) would be highly offensive to a reasonable person, and (b) is not of legitimate concern to the public."

11. The commentary to sec. 652D attempts to guide the determination of circumstances under which the publication of "private facts" can be subject to liability.

"In determining what is a matter of legitimate public interest, account must be taken of the customs and conventions of the community; and in the last analysis what is proper becomes a matter of the community mores. The line is to be drawn when the publicity ceases to be the giving of information to which the public is entitled, and becomes a morbid and sensational prying into private lives for its own sake, with which a reasonable member of the public, with decent standards, would say that he had no concern. The limitations, in other words, are those of common decency, having due regard to the freedom of the press and its reasonable leeway to choose what it will tell the public, but also due regard to the feelings of the individual and the harm that will be done to him by the exposure. Some reasonable proportion is also to be maintained between the event or activity that makes the individual a public figure and the private facts to which publicity is given." *Restatement of Torts, Second* (1965), sec. 652D, Comment h.

12. 413 U.S. 376 (1973).

13. Id. at 385.

14. See Anderson and Murdock, "Effects of Communication Law Decisions on Daily Newspaper Editors," 58 Journalism Quarterly 525 (1981); Anderson, Milner, and Galician, "How Editors

View Legal Issues and the Rehnquist Court," 65 Journalism Quarterly 294 (1988). The well-known *Associated Press Stylebook and Libel Manual* (Chicago: Addison-Wesley, 1987), self-described as "The Journalists' Bible," has a section devoted to summarizing the major Supreme Court decisions, and the law generally, on certain press freedoms. Id. at 292–312.

15. "The press needs the Court, if only for the simple reason that the Court is the ultimate guardian of the constitutional rights that support the press." Brennan, supra, 32 Rutg. L. Rev. at 174.

16. *New York Times Co. v. United States*, 403 U.S. 713 (1971).

17. Justice Brennan described an "extremely narrow class of cases in which the First Amendment's ban on prior judicial restraint may be overridden." Id. at 726. Such cases may only arise "when the Nation is at war" and the government can prove that publication will "inevitably, directly and immediately cause the occurrence" of an event that will jeopardize lives. Id. at 726-27.

Justice Stewart's standard of review was whether any of the documents "will surely result in direct, immediate, and irreparable damage to our Nation or its people." Id. at 730.

Justice White would put a "very heavy burden" on the government to warrant a prior restraint injunction. Id. at 731.

18. Justice Stewart, id. at 730. Justice White, id. at 733, 735–40. Justice Marshall, id. at 743–45.

19. Justice Stewart, id. at 730. Justice White, id. at 731, 733. Justice Marshall, id. at 742, 745–47.

20. See Steven Katz, "National Security Controls, Information, and Communication in the United States," 133 Cong. Rec. S 7105 (21 May 1987).

21. See, e.g., Franklin, "Good Names and Bad Law: A Critique of Libel Law and a Proposal," 18 U.S.F. L. Rev. 1, 10 (1983). "Juries may well be manifesting general community resentment [toward the press] by imposing liability when given the opportunity."

Goodale, "The *Tavoulareas* Jury Verdict Provides a Chilling Lesson for the Press," 1 Com. Law 6 (3 November 1983): "My own sense is that the public now harbors great resentment against the press and it is showing up in jury verdicts in libel cases. . . . An easy way to get even with institutions of this sort, which seems to be beyond the reach of ordinary Americans, is to vote huge libel verdicts against them."

22. *United States v. The Progressive, Inc.,* 467 F. Supp. 990 (W.D. Wisc. 1979). "One does not build a hydrogen bomb in the basement. However, the article could possibly provide sufficient information to allow a medium size nation to move faster in developing a hydrogen weapon. It could provide a ticket to by-pass blind alleys." Id. at 993.

Professor Thomas Emerson and I filed an amicus curiae brief in this case on behalf of Scientific American in which we argued that the prior restraint on the *Progressive* should not be granted.

23. "The *Progressive* case has created a dilemma for the American press. The magazine has not received the groundswell of support from newspapers around the country that often occurs in free press controversies. Some newspapers that have traditionally been in the forefront of First Amendment defenders have opposed the *Progressive*'s stance. 'It is the wrong issue, at the wrong time, in the wrong place,' *The Los Angeles Times* stated editorially. The *Washington Post* called it 'John Mitchell's dream case—the one the Nixon Administration was never lucky enough to get: a real First Amendment loser.' However, other papers praised the *Progressive*. The *St. Louis Post-Dispatch* stated, 'Although the danger from H-bombs is real enough, it will not be met by stifling a free press but by striving for disarmament.' When asked why there had not been stronger press support, the *Progressive*'s publisher replied, 'You mention the H-bomb and people are immediately immobilized—newspaper editors are not immune to that virus.'" New York Times, 30 April 1979.

In an editorial, the Washington Post argued that if the government was correct and the description of how to make the bomb had never before appeared in print, "the public-interest case against printing is strong." The Post found the Progressive's argument that the government was only trying to monopolize discussion of defense policy "wholly unpersuasive. You don't need this kind of information to discuss or understand policy questions on nuclear arms." Yet the Post hedged on the prior restraint question. "Once the door is open to advance judicial scrutiny of what the press may publish, it will never be closed. The loss will be immediately destructive."

The better course of action, according to the Post, would have been for the government to permit the Progressive to print the article, and for the Progressive "to face the consequences of violating the Atomic Energy Act." The Post doubted whether the Progressive, "or any other responsible publication, would print such material after the government has made as strong a showing of-proper secrecy and potential danger as it has in this case."

If the Progressive insisted on publishing the information, the Post urged a "negotiated settlement under which The Progressive publishes a revised version of its article, leaving out the details to which the government objects." This would have served the dual role of preventing "the establishment of a worse legal precedent than already exists" and also permitting the magazine to make one of its key points. Editorial, Washington Post, 18 March 1979.

U.S. News & World Report reported that "some editors fear that the case is a weak one for the press because of the sensitivity of the H-bomb issue. . . . Says one Midwestern editor: 'The Progressive is on a kamikaze mission, and all of us in the press are on board.'" U.S. News & World Report, 9 April 1979.

24. Harry Kalven, The Negro and the First Amendment (Chicago: University of Chicago Press, 1965), 6. "[A]s a thumbnail summary of the last two or three decades of speech issues in the Supreme Court, we may come to see the Negro as winning back for us the freedoms the Communists seem to have lost for us."

25. Alexander Bickel, The Morality of Consent (New Haven: Yale University Press, 1975), 60–61: "[T]he American press was freer before it won its battle with the government in New York Times Co. v. United States (Pentagon Papers case) in 1971 than after its victory. Before June 15, 1971, through its troubles of 1798, through one civil and two world wars and other wars, there had never been an effort by the federal government to censor a newspaper by attempting to impose a restraint prior to publication, directly or in litigation. The New York Times won its case, over the Pentagon Papers, but that spell was broken, and in a sense freedom was thus diminished."

26. 467 F. Supp. 990, 996. "A mistake in ruling against The Progressive will seriously infringe cherished First Amendment rights. . . . A mistake in ruling against the United States could pave the way for thermonuclear annihilation for us all."

27. The Chicago Tribune, the fourth largest paper in the country at the time, published verbatim an account of the H-bomb se-

crets on the day after the Justice Department announced that it was abandoning the *Progressive* case. Reuters, 18 September 1979.

In an editorial, the Washington Post announced the "dismal end" of the Progressive case: "Nobody won." The government failed to protect fundamental secrets, and the Progressive and the press as a whole failed to establish that "the government has misused its secrecy stamp."

"The primary lesson to be learned from this affair is the flimsiness of prior restraint as a way to prevent the disclosure of secret information. . . . The only real protections then available against publication of such secrets are the moral constraints felt by those into whose hands they have fallen or the deterring effect of the criminal provisions of the Atomic Energy Act and other laws. In this case, neither was sufficient to prevent publication—the former because too many people thought the government was carrying secrecy too far and the latter because some people, apparently including the editors of the *Press Connection* [a small Wisconsin newspaper that published the information], believe the government lacks either the will or the ability to prosecute." The Post worried that the decision not to prosecute "could well turn [the Atomic Energy Act's] deterring provisions into a sham." Editorial, Washington Post, 19 September 1979.

28. See Anderson and Murdock, "Effects of Communication Law Decisions on Daily Newspaper Editors." 58 Journalism Quarterly 525, 526 (1981).

A "Progress Report" from the publisher of the Wall Street Journal at the beginning of 1980 stated, "The Seventies were marked by serious setbacks to the First Amendment rights of all Americans to be kept fully informed about their government and society. The Eighties promise new threats to these rights." Advertisement, New York Times, 14 January 1980.

Syndicated columnist Jack Anderson speculated that the "open hostility of the courts toward the press . . . possibly has grown out of the private attitudes of Chief Justice Warren Burger." Detroit Free Press, 11 October 1978.

The president of the American Newspaper Publishers Association was concerned with *Zurcher v. Stanford Daily,* 436 U.S. 547 (1978). The opinion "puts a sledge hammer in the hands of those who would batter the American people's First Amendment rights." 44 Vital Speeches 722 (1978), quoted in Brennan, supra, 32 Rutg. L. Rev. at 178.

The press also reacted to *Herbert v. Lando,* 441 U.S. 153 (1979), in which the Court held that, in order to establish actual malice in a libel suit, a plaintiff may inquire into the editorial processes of those responsible for publication. The decision was labeled "judicial Agnewism" by the Washington Star, 20 April 1979. The Miami Herald said that *Herbert* was an example of the Court following "its anti-press course into what can only be called an Orwellian domain." 20 April 1979. The managing editor of the St. Louis Post-Dispatch stated that the opinion "has the potential of totally inhibiting the press to a degree seldom seen outside a dictatorial or fascist country." Birmingham News, 19 April 1979. William Leonard, president of CBS News, said *Herbert* denied constitutional protection to "the journalist's most precious possession—his mind, his thoughts and his editorial judgment." New York Times, 19 April 1979. Jack Landau, director of the Reporters Committee for Freedom of the Press, asserted that "the press will soon have lost the last constitutional shred of its editorial privacy and independence from the government." Times-Picayune (New Orleans), 20 April 1979. (All of the above are from Brennan, supra at 179–80.)

Tom Wicker wrote that *Herbert* "has undoubtedly 'chilled' the willingness of the press to go after and make public controversial material." New York Times, 20 April 1979.

One commentator suggested that the American press was more divided than it appeared about *Herbert.* "The spokesmen for the media were predictably outraged. But if I hear the younger reporters and editors accurately, they are about as divided as the Supreme Court—two-thirds for the majority decision . . . and one-third against." New York Times, 20 April 1979.

Lyle Denniston, "The Burger Court and the Press," in *The Burger Years: Rights and Wrongs in the Supreme Court, 1969–1986,* ed. Herman Schwartz (New York: Viking, 1987). Denniston argued that the press "has been forced to abandon its naivete about what a regime of law can do for press freedom. . . . Steadily, case by case, the Burger Court made it obvious that the First Amendment could do only limited service in protecting expression that wandered afield from 'public debate' or 'expression upon public questions,' in the phrasing of *Sullivan.*"

Denniston decried the ambiguity the Burger Court brought to the previous virgin territory of freedom of the press. "The press literally has no way of knowing how any story will be regarded when measured by legal norms: Is the individual involved a 'public figure' (or only a 'limited purpose public figure') or a 'private figure?' Is the subject matter of public or of private 'concern' or a mix of the two? Does it touch upon or relate in any way to 'the essence of self-government?'

"To journalists, it has become painfully clear that when law becomes a part of the editorial process, it has an inherently limited effect. And, contrary to the assumptions of the Supreme Court and the illusions of libel plaintiffs' lawyers, the limitation that it creates is not necessarily in the direction of fair, balanced, or even responsible journalism (whatever any one of those may mean in relation to a given story). Law can at most assume *safe* journalism: in the felt need to inhibit recklessness, law penalizes energetic journalism; in the search for an enforceable duty of care, it stifles legitimate experimentation; in the pursuit of propriety, it frustates creativity. The journalistic imagination is not merely chilled; it may well be frozen" (emphasis in original).

Sidney Zion, "Freedom of the Press: A Tale of Two Libel Theories," in *The Burger Years,* supra. Zion charged that the Burger Court had, in "an awesome trashing," done the press in. P. 45. "None of this would have happened under Earl Warren." P. 46.

See Thomas I. Emerson, "Freedom of the Press under the Burger Court," in *The Burger Court: The Counter-Revolution That Wasn't,* ed. Vincent Blasi (New Haven: Yale University Press, 1983), 1.

29. The landmark free press decisions during the Burger Court era include: *New York Times Co. v. U.S. (Pentagon Papers* case), 403 U.S. 713 (1971); *Nebraska Press Assoc. v. Stuart,* 427 U.S. 539 (1976) (free press/fair trial); *Miami Herald Publishing Co. v. Tornillo,* 418 U.S. 241 (1974) (public access regulation); *Gertz v. Robert Welch, Inc.,* 418 U.S. 323 (1974) (defamation); *Richmond Newspapers, Inc. v. Virginia,* 448 U.S. 555 (1980) (access to criminal trials); and *Cox Broadcasting Corp. v. Cohn,* 420 U.S. 469 (1975) (privacy). The press, on the other hand, was less than (though not wholly) unsuccessful in *Branzburg v. Hayes,* 408 U.S. 665 (1972) (reporter's privilege); and *Zurcher v. Stanford Daily,* 436 U.S. 547 (1978) (newsroom searches). The press, also, did not achieve as complete a protection in the libel area as many within the press desired. See, e.g., *Rosenbloom v. Metromedia, Inc.,* 403 U.S. 29 (1971); and *Time, Inc. v. Firestone,* 424 U.S. 448 (1976). For descriptions of these cases, the reader should return to ch. 1, supra.

30. Justice Brennan said in a 1979 address: "[P]resent attitudes

of the press toward the Supreme Court strongly suggest the complete absence of an enterprise shared by the press and the Supreme Court. Surely there is reason for that doubt when a respected and influential newspaper labels the Court's work of last Term 'a virtual disaster,' and others charge that the Court has engaged in a 'relentless assault' on the press, that it is 'dismantling' the First Amendment. The press, of course, has in the past disagreed with rulings of the Court, but I detect in the present controversy a new and disturbing note of acrimony, almost bitterness." 32 Rutg. L. Rev. at 174.

31. 418 U.S. 241, 249 (1974).

32. Id. at 240.

33. Id. at 254.

34. Another example of what I am calling the schizophrenic character of the Burger Court decisions, with strong pro-press results and undermining rhetoric in the opinions, is the *Nebraska Press* case. As noted in Chapter 1, that decision affirmed the First Amendment right of the press to comment on an ongoing criminal trial, at least without fear of facing a judicial injunction. Yet, in announcing this important victory for press freedom, Chief Justice Burger's opinion for the Court utilized a test that had been widely discredited as insufficiently sensitive to free speech and press values. For an account of this extraordinary event, see Schmidt, "*Nebraska Press Association:* An Expansion of Freedom and Contraction of Theory," 29 Stanford L. Rev. 431, 458–66 (1977).

35. *Branzburg v. Hayes,* 408 U.S. at 665 (1972).

36. Vincent Blasi, "The Checking Value in First Amendment Theory," 1977 Am. Bar Found. Res. J. 521, 593 (1977).

37. Id.

38. Justice White, concurring in *Rosenbloom,* supra: "Some members of the Court seemed haunted by fears of self-censorship by the press and of damage judgments that will threaten its financial health. But technology has immeasurably increased the power of the press to do both good and evil. Vast communication combines have been built into profitable ventures. My interest is not in protecting the treasuries of communicators but in implementing the First Amendment by insuring that effective communication which is essential to the continued functioning of our free society." 403 U.S. at 60.

39. See Spiro Agnew, "Speeches on the Media," in *Killing the Messenger, 100 Years of Media Criticism,* ed. Tom Goldstein (New York: Columbia University Press, 1989), 64.

40. See Neil Postman, *Amusing Ourselves to Death: Public Discourse in the Age of Show Business* (New York: Penguin, 1985); Walter Goodman, "Is Network News Pushing to Do Less?" New York Times, 8 February 1990; Sandra Salmans, "TV's Newscasters Give Low Marks to Newcomers," New York Times, 15 April 1984, sec. 2.

41. 418 U.S. at 259.

42. Id. at 261.

43. "[S]ome Americans firmly believe that the former Vice President and the former President of the United States were hounded out of office by an arrogant and irresponsible press that had outrageously usurped dictatorial power. . . . It is my thesis this morning that, on the contrary, the established American press in the past ten years, and particularly in the past two years, has performed precisely the function it was intended to perform by those who wrote the First Amendment of our Constitution." Stewart, "Or of the Press," 26 Hastings L. J. 631 (1975).

"As money is to the economy, so the press is to our political culture: it is the medium of circulation. It is the currency through which the knowledge of recent events is exchanged; the coin by which *public* discussion may be purchased." Brennan, supra, 32 Rutg. L. Rev. at 175 (emphasis in original).

44. Stewart, supra: "The primary purpose of the constitutional guarantee of a free press was . . . to create a fourth institution outside the government as an additional check on the three official branches. . . . The relevant metaphor . . . is of the Fourth Estate." 26 Hastings L. J. at 634.

"[T]he Free Press guarantee is, in essence, a *structural* provision of the Constitution. Most of the other provisions in the Bill of Rights protect specific liberties or specific rights of individuals. . . . In contrast, the Free Press Clause extends protection to an institution." Id. at 633 (emphasis in original).

"[The structural model of the press] focuses on the relationship of the press to the communicative functions required by our democratic beliefs. To the extent the press makes these functions possible, this model requires that it receive the protection of the First Amendment. A good example is the press's role in providing and circulating the information necessary for informed public discussion. To the extent the press, or, for that matter, to the extent that any institution uniquely performs this role, it should receive unique First Amendment protection." Brennan, 32 Rutg. L. Rev. at 177. For criticism of the Supreme Court's view of the institutional role of the press, see Denniston, in *The Burger Years,* at 34–44.

45. See, e.g., Dworkin, "Is the Press Losing the First Amendment?" New York Review of Books, 4 December 1980, 49, 51–52.

46. Justice Brennan has asserted: "The decisions that have aroused the sharpest controversy between the Court and the press have been those decisions in which the Court has tried to wrestle with the constitutional implications of this structural model of the press. . . . [T]he press, in order to strengthen its rhetorical position, insisted on treating [*Branzburg* and *Zurcher*] exactly as if they involved only the traditional model of the press as public spokesman. . . . The tendency of the press to confuse these two models has, in my opinion, been at the root of much of the recent acrimony in press-Court relations. The press has reacted as if its role as a public spokesman were being restricted, and, as a consequence, it has on occasion over-reacted." 32 Rutg. L. Rev. at 177–78.

47. See, e.g., Nimmer, "Is Freedom of the Press a Redundancy?" 26 Hastings L. J. 639 (1975); Lange, "The Speech and Press Clauses," 23 UCLA L. Rev. 77 (1975); "Symposium on the Press Clause," 7 Hofstra L. Rev. 559 (1979); Van Alstyne, "The Hazards to the Press of Claiming a 'Preferred Position,'" 28 Hastings L. J. 761 (1977).

48. See "Journalism Educators Debate Strategies, Technology and Ties to the Media," New York Times, 23 January 1984; T. Goldstein, *The News at Any Cost* (New York: Simon and Schuster, 1985), 155–83; H. Goodwin, *Groping for Ethics in Journalism* (Ames: Iowa State University Press, 1983), 50–55.

49. See, e.g., Dworkin, "Is the Press Losing the First Amendment?" supra.

50. Commission on Freedom of the Press, *A Free and Responsible Press* (Chicago: University of Chicago Press, 1947), 121.

51. See *New York Times Co. v. Sullivan,* 376 U.S. 272, 273 n.13, 305 (1964).

52. See M. Schudson, *Discovering the News: A Social History of American Newspapers* (New York: Basic Books, 1978), 160–94.

53. An admittedly slight but interesting piece of data on changes in the twentieth-century self-image of the press (or its self-presentation) is to be found in the codes of ethics. One of the most prominent is that of the Society of Professional Journalists (Sigma Delta Chi). Its first code, adopted in 1926, articulates the function of the press in terms of serving the "human race" ("The primary function of newspapers is to communicate to the human race what its members do, feel and think") and "mankind" ("Freedom of the Press is to be guarded as a vital right of mankind"). The most recent (1987) version describes the role of the press, in a democratic political context, as the representative of the public. Thus "agencies of mass communication" become "carriers of public discussion and information, acting on their Constitutional mandate and freedom to learn and report the facts," thereby fulfilling "the public's right to know the truth" and "of events of public importance and interest." A function of freedom of the press is "to discuss, question, and challenge actions and utterances of our government and our public and private institutions."

CHAPTER FOUR

1. Radio Act of 1927, ch. 169, 44 Stat. 1162.

2. Communications Act of 1934, Title 3, ch. 56, 48 Stat. 1081, as amended by 47 U.S.C. sections 301–95 (1988).

3. Id. sec. 303.

4. Id. sec. 326.

5. Id. sec. 309(a), 3 F.C.C. Rcd. 5467 (1988).

6. Developed over the years under the commission's general power to promulgate regulations consistent with the "public interest," 47 U.S.C. sections 303, 307 (1970), the fairness doctrine requires broadcasters to provide adequate and fair coverage of opposing viewpoints on controversial issues of public importance. The substance of these obligations was set forth in early commission decisions. See *Great Lakes Broadcasting Co.,* 3 F.R.C. Ann. Rep. 32, 33 (1929), *revd. on other grounds,* 37 F.2d 993 (D.C. Cir. 1930), *cert dismissed,* 281 U.S. 706; *Trinity Methodist Church, South v. F.R.C.,* 62 F.2d 850 (D.C. Cir. 1932), *cert. denied,* 288 U.S. 599 (1933). However, the first official policy statement explaining the doctrine in detail was not issued by the commission until 1949. See Report on Editorializing by Broadcast Licensees, 13 F.C.C. 1246 (1949). Congressional endorsement of the doctrine followed ten years later.

Act of September 14, 1959, Pub. L. no. 86-274, sec. 1, 73 Stat. 557, *amending* 47 U.S.C. sec. 315(a) (1958) (codified at 47 U.S.C. sec. 315(a) (1988); see *Red Lion Broadcasting Co. v. F.C.C.*, 395 U.S. 367, 380–82 (1969).

As noted in the text, the broadcast media has been subject to extensive legal restraints since the passage of the Radio Act in 1927. Congress acted that year in response to a massive problem of signal interference, which threatened the continued existence of the new technology, and "under the spur of a widespread fear that in the absence of governmental control the public interest might be subordinated to monopolistic domination in the broadcastingt field." *F.C.C. v. Pottsville Broadcasting Co.*, 309 U.S. 134, 137 (1940). Within the space of about a decade, radio had grown in popularity and social importance to such an extent that intervention became necessary to facilitate allocation of the small number of available frequencies. Congress delegated this responsibility to the Federal Radio Commission, vesting it with the authority to issue licenses and promulgate regulations consistent with the public "convenience, interest, or necessity." Radio Act of 1927, ch. 169, sec. 4, 44 Stat. 1163. The Federal Communications Act was passed in 1934, but, aside from renaming the commission, the essential nature of radio regulation was left unchanged. Communications Act of 1934, Title 3, ch. 56, 48 Stat. 1081, as amended by forty-seven U.S.C. sections 301–95 (1988). The professed object of the new enterprise remained to "make available, so far as possible, to all the people of the United States a rapid, efficient, Nation-wide, and worldwide wire and radio communication service." 47 U.S.C. sec. 151 (1988).

7. 11 C.F.R. sec. 73.1920 (1990).

8. 11 C.F.R. sec. 73.1930 (1990).

9. Communications Act of 1934, Title 3, ch. 56, 48 Stat. 1081 (current version at 47 U.S.C. sec. 315 [1988]).

10. The full text of sec. 315 reads as follows:

"(a) Equal opportunities requirement; censorship prohibition; allowance of station use; news appearances exception; public interest; public issues discussion opportunities.

"If any licensee shall permit any person who is a legally qualified candidate for any public office to use a broadcasting station, he shall afford equal opportunities to all other such candidates for that office in the use of such broadcasting station: *Provided,* That such licensee shall have no power of censorship over the material broadcast under the provisions of this section. No obligation is imposed under this subsection upon any licensee to allow the use of its station by any such candidate. Appearance by a legally qualified candidate on any—(1) bona fide newscast, (2) bona fide news interview, (3) bona fide news documentary (if the appearance of the candidate is incidental to the presentation of the subject or subjects covered by the news documentary), or (4) on-the-spot coverage of bona fide news events (including but not limited to political conventions and activities incidental thereto), shall not be deemed to be use of a broadcasting station within the meaning of this subsection. Nothing in the foregoing sentence shall be construed as relieving broadcasters, in connection with the presentation of newscasts, news interviews, news documentaries, and on-the-spot coverage of news events, from the obligation imposed upon them under this chapter to operate in the public interest and to afford reasonable opportunity for the discussion of conflicting views on issues of public importance.

(b) Broadcast media rates.

The charges made for the use of any broadcasting station by any person who is a legally qualified candidate for any public office in connection with his campaign for nomination for election, or election to such office shall not exceed—(1) during the forty-five days preceding the date of a primary or primary runoff election and during the sixty days preceding the date of a general or special election in which such person is a candidate, the lowest unit charge of the station for the same class and amount of time for the same period; and (2) at any other time, the charges made for comparable use of such station by other users thereof.

(c) Definitions.

For purposes of this section—(1) the term "broadcasting station" includes a community antenna television system; and (2) the terms "licensee" and "station licensee" when used with respect to a community antenna television system mean the operator of such system.

(d) Rules and regulations.

The Commission shall prescribe appropriate rules and regulations to carry out the provisions of this section. 47 U.S.C. sec. 315 (1988).

11. Id., sec. 312(a)(7) (1988).

12. CBS program "Hunger in America," 20 F.C.C.2d 143, 151 (1969).

13. *Federal Communications Commission v. Pacifica Foundation,* 438 U.S. 726 (1978).

14. See *Zenith Radio Corp.,* 40 F.C.C.2d 223, 231 (1973); *Primer on* "Ascertainment of Community Problems by Broadcast Applicants," 27 F.C.C.2d 650, 679–80 (1971). Subsequently, the commission declined to review format changes, a position upheld by the Supreme Court in *F.C.C. v. WNCN Listeners Guild,* 450 U.S. 582 (1981).

15. 319 U.S. 190 (1943).

16. The broadcasters in *National Broadcasting Co. v. United States,* id., challenged on statutory and constitutional grounds the so-called chain broadcasting regulations, designed by the commission to regulate various aspects of a network's relationship with its affiliated stations. See id. at 198–209.

17. Id. at 226–27.

18. *Red Lion Broadcasting Co. v. Federal Communications Commission,* 395 U.S. at 367, 371.

19. Fred W. Friendly, *The Good Guys, the Bad Guys and the First Amendment: Free Speech vs. Fairness in Broadcasting* (New York: Random House, 1975).

20. 395 U.S. 367 (1969).

21. Id. at 386.

22. Id.

23. Id. at 387.

24. Id. at 388.

25. Id.

26. Id.

27. Id. at 389.

28. 412 U.S. 94 (1973).

29. Id. at 124.

30. 412 U.S. 94 (1973) (Justice Brennan and Justice Marshall dissenting).

31. 453 U.S. 367 (1981).

32. Id. at 395 (quoting *Office of Communication of the United Church of Christ v. F.C.C.*, 359 F.2d 994 (D.C. Cir. 1966).

33. Id. at 397.

34. 395 U.S. at 389.

35. Id. at 390.

36. Id.

37. Id.

38. Id.

39. Id. at 393.

40. Id. at 399.

41. *In re Complaint of Representative Patsy Mink*, 59 F.C.C.2d 987 (1976).

42. Id. at 996.

43. Id.

44. Id. at 996–97.

45. Id. at 995.

46. 405 F.2d 1082 (D.C. Cir. 1968), *cert. denied*, 396 U.S. 842 (1969).

47. Id. at 1086.

48. Id.

49. Id. at 1096.

50. Id. at 1097.

51. Id.

52. Id. at 1098–99.

53. Id. at 1100–1101.

54. Id. at 1101 n.77.

55. 516 F.2d 1101 (D.C. Cir. 1974).

56. Id. at 1107.

57. Id. at 1127–30.

58. *Green v. F.C.C.*, 447 F.2d 323 (D.C. Cir. 1971).

59. *Friends of the Earth v. F.C.C.*, 449 F.2d 1164 (D.C. Cir. 1971).

60. "The Handling of Public Issues under the Fairness Doc-

trine and the Public Interest Standards of the Communications Act," 48 F.C.C.2d 1, 23 (1974).

61. *Public Interest Research Group v. F.C.C.*, 522 F.2d 1060 (1st Cir. 1975), *cert. denied*, 424 U.S. at 965.

62. Public Health Cigarette Smoking Act of 1969, ch. 36, 79, Stat. 283. Current version at 15 U.S.C. sec. 1335 (1988).

63. *Larus & Brother Co., Inc. v. F.C.C.*, 447 F.2d 876 (4th Cir. 1971).

64. *National Broadcasting Co. v. F.C.C.*, 516 F.2d 1101 (D.C. Cir. 1974).

65. See Syracuse Peace Council, 99 F.C.C.2d 1389 (1984).

66. General Fairness Doctrine, Obligations of Broadcast Licensees, 102 F.C.C.2d 143 (1985).

67. In *Telecommunications Research and Action Center v. F.C.C.*, 801 F.2d 501 (D.C. Cir. 1986), the court of appeals held that the fairness doctrine had not been codified by Congress, leaving it open to the commission to decide whether to abandon the doctrine, as the commission in its 1985 report had indicated it would like to do. Congress then enacted legislation codifying the fairness doctrine, but it was quickly vetoed by President Reagan. Following that, the commission formally repealed the fairness doctrine. See Syracuse Peace Council, 2 F.C.C.Rcd. 5043 (1987). That discussion was upheld by the D.C. Circuit, without reaching constitutional issues. *Syracuse Peace Council v. F.C.C.*, 867 F.2d 654 (1989). Congressional efforts to codify the fairness doctrine continue in both Houses, but to date without complete success.

CHAPTER FIVE

1. See, e.g., Fowler, "The Public's Interest," 61 Fla. Bar J. 213 (1982); Krattenmaker and Powe, "The Fairness Doctrine Today: A Constitutional Curiosity and an Impossible Dream," 1985 Duke L. J. 151; Powe, *American Broadcasting and the First Amendment* (Berkeley: University of California Press, 1987).

2. See, e.g., Owen M. Fiss, "Why the State?" 100 Harv. L. Rev. 781 (1987).

3. *National Broadcasting Co., Inc. v. U.S.*, 319 U.S. 190, 226 (1943).

4. *Red Lion Broadcasting Co. v. F.C.C.*, 395 U.S. 367, 386 (1969).

5. Id. at 388.

6. Id.

7. Id. at 389.

8. Id. at 390.

9. Id.

10. See, e.g., *Columbia Broadcasting Sys., Inc. v. Democratic Natl. Comm.*, 412 U.S. 94, 101, 126 (1973). See also *F.C.C. v. League of Women Voters*, 468 U.S. 364 (1984).

11. Bollinger, "Freedom of the Press and Public Access: Toward a Theory of Partial Regulation of the Mass Media," 75 Mich. L. Rev. 1 (1976).

12. Kalven, "Broadcasting, Public Policy and the First Amendment," 10 J. Law & Econ. 15, 16 (1967).

13. Id. at 24.

14. See Z. Chafee, *Government and Mass Communications* (Chicago: University of Chicago Press, 1947), 638.

15. See Commission on Freedom of the Press, *A Free and Responsible Press* (Chicago: University of Chicago Press, 1947), 82–83.

16. See A. Meiklejohn, *Free Speech and Its Relation to Self-Government* (New York: Harper & Bros., 1948), 99.

17. See W. Douglas, *The Right of the People* (New York: Doubleday, 1958), 76–77. Justice Douglas changed his mind by the time of his concurring opinion in *Columbia Broadcasting Sys., Inc. v. Democratic Natl. Comm.*, 412 U.S. 94, 154 (Justice Douglas concurring).

18. Justice Black joined the unanimous Court in *Red Lion Broadcasting Co. v. Federal Communications Commission*, 395 U.S. 367 (1969).

19. See T. Emerson, *The System of Freedom of Expression* (New York: Random House, 1970), 653–67.

20. See, e.g., N. Dowling and G. Gunther, *Cases and Materials on Constitutional Law*, 7th ed. (Mineola: Foundation Press 1965).

21. See, e.g., the two-page note on *Red Lion* in Gunther and Dowling, id. at 1225–26 (8th ed., 1970); W. Lockhart, Y. Kamisar, and J. Choper, *Constitutional Law: Cases and Materials*, 975–79, 1201–10, 4th ed. (St. Paul: West Publishing Co., 1975).

In the ninth edition of the Gunther casebook, published in 1975, *Red Lion* and *CBS* are described in a three-page textual comment and *Tornillo* immediately afterward in a two-page note. G. Gunther, *Cases and Materials on Constitutional Law,* 1230–34 (Mineola: Foundation Press, 1975).

Currently, casebooks give somewhat more treatment to public regulation of electronic media, but it still seems remarkably slight. The eleventh edition of the Gunther casebook, for example, devotes approximately fifteen pages to broadcast and cable regulation out of 489 pages on freedom of speech and press. G. Gunther, *Constitutional Law,* 11th ed. (Mineola: Foundation Press, 1985). In the 1990 supplement it is four of 167 pages. In another widely used casebook, the coverage is somewhat greater: thirty-nine out of 398 pages in the basic textbook and six out of 166 pages in the 1990 supplement. W. Lockhart, Y. Kamisar, J. Choper, S. Shiffrin, *Constitutional Law,* 6th ed. (St. Paul: West Publishing Co., 1986).

22. Hutchins, "Foreword" to Commission on Freedom of the Press, *A Free and Responsible Press,* at v.

23. Commission on Freedom of the Press, *A Free and Responsible Press,* supra n.15 at 82.

24. Id. at 82–83.

25. Coase, "Evaluation of Public Policy Relating to Radio and Television Broadcasting: Social and Economic Issues," 41 J. Land & P.U. Econ. 161 (1965). See also Coase, *The Federal Communications Commission,* 2 J. Law & Econ. 1 (1959).

26. Id. at 40.

27. T. Emerson, *The System of Freedom of Expression,* at 667.

28. Barron, "Access to the Press—A New First Amendment Right," 80 Harv. L. Rev. 1641 (1967).

29. See Barron, "An Emerging First Amendment Right of Access to the Media?" 37 Geo. Wash. L. Rev. 487 (1969); Barron, "Access—the Only Choice for the Media?" 48 Tex. L. Rev. 766 (1970).

30. 453 U.S. 367 (1981). See also *Metro Broadcasting, Inc. v. F.C.C.,* 110 S. Ct. 2997 (1990).

31. A small piece of evidence supporting the potential influence of the fairness doctrine on the print media is the change over the years in the concept of "fair play" in the Society of Professional Journalists' Code of Ethics. The 1926 version of the code recognized the rule that "news media should not communicate unofficial

charges affecting reputation or moral character without opportunity given to the accused to be heard." The most recent version (in 1987) repeats that rule but expands the "fair play" concept to include the injunction that "[j]ournalists should be accountable to the public for their reports and the public should be encouraged to voice its grievances against the media. Open dialogue with our readers, viewers, and listeners should be fostered."

32. The observation that the character of print journalism has changed, becoming more of a "common carrier" of news as the medium has assumed monopolistic status, out of a wise self-recognition of society's demands of fairness in communications monopolies, has also been made by I. Pool, *Technologies of Freedom* (Cambridge, Mass.: Harvard University Press, 1983), 238–39.

33. *Red Lion* was decided in June 1969. The New York Times began the Op. Ed. page on 21 September 1970. The editorial introducing the new page stated that the "purpose of the Op. Ed. page is neither to reinforce nor to counterbalance The Times' own editorial position" but rather "to afford greater opportunity for exploration of issues and presentation of new insights and new ideas by writers and thinkers who have no institutional connection with The Times and whose views will very frequently be completely divergent from our own." New York Times, 21 September 1970, at 42.

34. "The greatest obstacle to the development of a vigorous tradition of freedom of speech in broadcasting may well have been the placidity and the decency of the FCC. The Commission has claimed the widest powers, but it has exercised them with discouraging circumspection." Kalven, "Broadcasting, Public Policy and the First Amendment," 10 J. Law & Econ. 15, 18 (1967).

35. 334 U.S. 131.

36. Cf. I. Pool, *Technologies of Freedom,* at 239–40.

37. *CATV and TV Reporters Services,* 26 F.C.C. 403, 429 (1959).

38. See *Carter Mountain Transmission Corp.,* 32 F.C.C. 459 (1963), affirmed, 321 F.2d 359 (D.C. Cir. 1963).

39. First Report and Order, 38 F.C.C. 683, 716–19 (1965). The commission allowed an exception for situations in which substantial duplication would result. Id. at 717.

40. Id. at 438.

41. Second Report and Order, 2 F.C.C.2d 725, 728–34, 781–85 (1966).

42. 392 U.S. 157 (1968).

43. Id. at 173.

44. Id. at 167; 47 U.S.C. sec. 152(a) (1976). Cable systems operate by receiving the signals of television stations, amplifying them, transmitting them by wire or microwave, and ultimately distributing them by wire (the "cable") to the receivers of their subscribers. Id. at 161.

45. Id. at 173, quoting *National Broadcasting Co. v. U.S.*, 319 U.S. 190, 219 (1943).

46. Id. at 174–75.

47. Id. at 178.

48. This view was first advocated in Note, "Cable Television and the First Amendment," 71 Colum. L. Rev. 1008 (1971). See also Note, "The Proposed Cable Communications Act of 1975: A Recommendation for Comprehensive Regulation," 93 Duke L. J. 93, 112–13 (1975).

49. The rule provided that "no CATV (cable) system having 3,500 or more subscribers shall carry the signal of any television broadcast station unless the system also operates to a significant extent as a local outlet by cablecasting and has available facilities for local production and presentation of programs other than automated services." 47 C.F.R. sec. 74.1111(a) (1973), revised as 47 C.F.R. sec. 76.201(a) (1973). In fact, this regulation was suspended soon after its promulgation and eventually abandoned altogether by the commission in 1974. See Federal Register, vol. 39 (1974), 43, 302.

50. 406 U.S. 649 (1972).

51. Id. at 655 n.10.

52. Id. at 670.

53. Id. at 664.

54. Id. at 676.

55. Id. at 679–80.

56. Id. at 664; see also id. at 667, where Brennan says: "In short, the regulatory authority . . . sustained by this Court in *South-*

western was authority to regulate . . . [cable] with a view not merely to protect but to promote the objectives for which the Commission had been assigned jurisdiction over broadcasting."

57. 440 U.S. 689 (1979).

58. Id. at 691–93, 701–2.

59. Sec. 3(h) circularly defines a "common carrier" as "any person engaged as a common carrier for hire, in interstate or foreign communication by wire or radio or interstate or foreign radio transmission of energy." 47 U.S.C. sec. 3(h) (1976).

60. *F.C.C. v. Midwest Video Corp.*, supra n.57 at 707.

61. Id. at 709 n.19.

62. 47 U.S.C. 531 (1988).

63. *City of Los Angeles v. Preferred Communications, Inc.*, 476 U.S. 488 (1986).

64. The Court stated: "Cable television partakes of some of the aspects of speech and the communication of ideas as do the traditional enterprises of newspaper and book publishers, public speakers, and pamphleteers." *City of Los Angeles v. Preferred Communications, Inc.*, 476 U.S. at 494.

On remand the district court has just recently decided against the city. Judge Consuelo Marshall conceived of cable television as "in between the broadcast media and print media on the governmental regulation continuum, however closer to the print media." Memorandum Order, Case no. CV-83-5846 (5 January 1990) (unpublished), 19. Judge Marshall reasoned: "The programming of a cable television network, like the publishing of a newspaper, involves editorial discretion. Moreover, unlike broadcast, cable television does not require use of the airwaves. However, the Court recognizes the potential for disruption of the public domain inherent in stringing coaxial cables along the City's utility poles and conduits." Id. at 18.

I participated as an expert witness on behalf of the City of Los Angeles.

65. *Public Television: A Program for Action, The Report and Recommendations of the Carnegie Commission on Educational Television* (New York: Bantam, 1967), 15–16.

66. The National Association of Broadcasters filed amicus curiae briefs in *Capital Cities Cable, Inc. v. Crisp*, 467 U.S. 691 (1984), in which the Court struck down, as preempted by federal statutory

law, an Oklahoma law prohibiting cable television systems from retransmitting out-of-state transmissions of alcohol commercials, and in *City of Los Angeles v. Preferred Communications, Inc.*, 476 U.S. 488 (1986).

67. The Carnegie Commission Report began with a quotation from E. B. White, which became a classic statement of the purposes of public television:

> Noncommercial television should address itself to the ideal of excellence, not the idea of acceptability—which is what keeps commercial television from climbing the staircase. I think television should be the visual counterpart of the literary essay, should arouse our dreams, satisfy our hunger for beauty, take us on journeys, enable us to participate in events, present great drama and music, explore the sea and the sky and the woods and the hills. It should be our Lyceum, our Chautauqua, our Minsky's, and our Camelot. It should restate and clarify the social dilemma and the political pickle. Once in a while it does, and you get a quick glimpse of its potential. (*Public Television: A Program for Action, The Report and Recommendations of the Carnegie Commission on Educational Television* [New York: Bantam, 1967], 13).

Later in the report, White's vision is expanded in language that echoes the Hutchins commission report:

> With difficulties realistically in mind, and with an acute awareness of the hazards inherent in discussing illustrative examples drawn from a program field as wide in scope and diverse in possibility as that of Public Television, we offer the following general observations with regard to the opportunities that will exist for Public Television programming.
>
> Public Television programming can deepen a sense of community in local life. It should show us our community as it really is. It should be a forum for debate and controversy. It should bring into the home meetings, now generally untelevised, where major public decisions are hammered out, and occasions where people of the community express their hopes, their protests, their enthusiasms, and their will. It should provide a voice for groups in the community that may otherwise be unheard.
>
> Public Television programs can help us see America whole, in all its diversity. To a degree unequaled by any other me-

dium, Public Television should be a mirror of the American style. It should remind us of our heritage and enliven our traditions. Its programs should draw on the full range of emotion and mood, from the comic to the tragic, that we know in American life. It should help us look at our achievements and difficulties, at our conflicts and agreements, at our problems, and at the far reach of our possibilities. Public Television programs should help us know what it is to be many in one, to have growing maturity in our sense of ourselves as a people.

Public Television can increase our understanding of the world, of other nations and cultures, of the whole commonwealth of man. Public Television programs should keep pace, in their attention to world affairs, with the revolutionary technology that is making every part of the world instantaneously accessible to every other part. Through Public Television programs, and through advances in the technology of communication, Americans should have rapidly increasing opportunities for greater insight into the nature of other nations and cultures, for a clearer understanding of struggles and settlements between nations, for a view far beyond our own borders into the ways of the rest of the world. Public Television programs should take us into other traditions, should expose us to other histories, should let us see how we and the world look from other vantage points on the globe, and should let us reflect on the quiet achievements, raging crises, and the joys and pains of ordinary life elsewhere in the world.

Public Television can open a wide door to greater expression and cultural richness for creative individuals and important audiences. It should seek out able people whose talents might otherwise not be known and shared. The search for new or unrecognized ability should include but not be limited to conventional ideas of talent. There should be a search for the unusual, for the commonplace skill uncommonly mastered, for the rare personality, for the familiar expressing itself in new ways.

Public Television programs should show us domains of learning, emotion, and doing, examples of skill, human expressiveness, and physical phenomena that might otherwise be outside our ken. It should bring to us new knowledge and skills, lifting our sights, providing us with relaxation and recreation, and bringing before us glimpses of greatness. Public Television programs should have the means to be daring, to break away from narrow convention, to be human and earthy. Public Television programming should explore new dimensions of artistic performance not ordinarily available to our nation's audiences. It should present important playwrights whose work is too seldom performed. It should give a stage to experimental drama, to the work of promising young playwrights in search of an audience. It should provide a vehicle for the best of the yet unknown actors and actresses, a concert stage for unknown but talented musical artists. It should encourage and use films that display vital originality. It should promote further experimentation in choreography, pantomime, music, drama, lighting, staging, and all aspects of artistic and dramatic presentation in terms of television. Without lowering its aims, Public Television can be marked by exuberance or naturalness or simplicity, reaching for the things that make the world kin, that join together reality and delight.

Public Television can be powerfully educational, even when it is not presenting formal instruction. Public Television programs should carry the best of knowledge and wisdom directly into the home. Great teachers should have opportunities to interpret the new math, the new physics, the new social sciences through home television. Some of the best educational films of the past decade were made as teaching aids to new curricula. They should be adapted to television.

The unique opportunity is to bring before those who seek to understand, those who understand deeply. Public Television should give each home the opportunity to be a center for learning, where knowledge and scholarship are informally and expertly available. Public Television has already demonstrated its capacity to be responsive to the people's hunger for knowledge and self-improvement, but it is only at the threshold of what might be done.

. . . Public Television can extend our knowledge and understanding of contemporary affairs. Its programming of the news should grow to encompass both facts and meaning, both information and interpretation. It should be historian, in addition to being daily journalist. Its programs should call upon the intellectual resources of the nation to give perspective and depth to interpretation of the news, in addition to coverage of news day by day. This enlarged canvas should show us the interplay of people and events, in terms of time and place, history and consequence. Programming in contemporary affairs should be sensitive to the long groundswells of civilization as well as to its earthquakes.

Public Television's programs should search out the influences that different fields have on each other, looking at the relationships between science and politics, art and therapy, technology and agriculture, psychology and warfare, outer space and international relations. Programs should assess the broad significance of a news item: the mine disaster, the Supreme Court decision, the new tax, the labor strike, the scientific discovery. The bare reporting of incidents is not sufficient to meet the responsibilities we see for Public Television. Programs should find ways to show us the context of incidents, the past and present from which they spring, the impact they may make on tomorrow.

Public Television can serve Americans by providing analysis of much more than the events of current history. Just as there is a scarcity of thorough analysis and interpretation of the news, there is an even greater scarcity of television analysis of forms and ideas in art and philosophy, in music and literature, in science and technology, and in other fields of human expression and endeavor. With rare exceptions, such analysis as one finds is limited to the narrow confines of the panel discussion, the interview, or the formal lecture. Much greater imaginativeness and inventiveness are needed in programming for the analysis of forms and ideas. Public Television programs should be much more than a crude public stage for such presentation. With freedom and imagination, Public Television programming should be an innovative laboratory for the analysis of the intellectual, artistic, and social substance of our culture. (Id. at 92–96)

These ideas about the role of public television in raising the level of public discussion about social and intellectual issues were repeated in the Congressional Committee reports leading up to the enactment of the Public Broadcasting Act. See, e.g., 1967 U.S. Code Congressional & Administrative News 1772–75, 1801–2.

CHAPTER SIX

1. Lee Bollinger, "Freedom of the Press and Public Access: Toward a Theory of Partial Regulation of the Mass Media," 75 Mich. L. Rev. 1 (1976).

2. Z. Chafee, *Free Speech in the United States* (Cambridge, Mass.: Harvard University Press, 1941; rpt. New York: Atheneum, 1969), 559 (all references are to later printing).

3. See, e.g., T. Emerson, *The System of Freedom of Expression* (New York: Random House, 1970), ch. 17; Reich, "The Law of the Planned Society," 75 Yale L. J. 1227 (1966).

4. 326 U.S. 1 (1945).

5. Id. at 20.

6. See *Marsh v. Alabama*, 326 U.S. 501; *Amalgamated Food Employees v. Logan Valley Plaza, Inc.*, 391 U.S. 308 (1968). But see *Hudgens v. NLRB*, 424 U.S. 507 (1976); *Lloyd Corp. v. Tanner*, 407 U.S. 551 (1972).

7. An interesting response to the problem of access in the mass media has been the noticeable solicitude for minor modes of communication. Judicial opinions and scholarly commentary have emphasized the need for protection of these methods of communication precisely because of the restricted nature of the press. See, e.g., *Martin v. Struthers*, 319 U.S. 141, 146 (1943) ("Door to door distribution of circulars is essential to the poorly financed causes of little people"); *Kovacs v. Cooper*, 336 U.S. 77, 98 (1949) (Justice Black dissenting). See also Kalven, "The Concept of the Public Forum: Cox v. Louisiana," 1965 Sup. Ct. Rev. 1, 30; Stone, "Fora Americana: Speech in Public Places," 1974 Sup. Ct. Rev. 233, 233–34. Though important, this is hardly an adequate response to the problem of concentration in the mass media.

8. Other major attempts at reform have come primarily in the area of antitrust law. The Newspaper Preservation Act, Pub. L. no. 91-353, 84 Stat. 466 (1970) (codified at 15 U.S.C. sec. 1801–4 (1970), which permits competing newspapers under certain circumstances to merge under a so-called joint operating agreement, is an example of the use of the antitrust laws to foster opportunities for debate within the press. However, it also represents a recognition that the antitrust laws themselves are not likely to achieve more diversity of outlets since the high economies of scale in the newspaper industry seem to lead to the creation of natural monopolies. See B. Schmidt, *Freedom of the Press v. Public Access* (New York: Praeger, 1976), 51–54.

On a private level, one might note the recent formation of the National News Council. The council is a mediating organization with no powers of enforcement. For a description of its operation and an analysis of the effectiveness of this and other press councils, see Ritter and Leibowitz, "Press Councils: The Answer to Our First Amendment Dilemma," 1974 Duke L. J. 845. (See also n.40 in ch. 2, supra.)

9. For evaluations of the chilling effect of access regulation, see Lange, "The Role of the Access Doctrine in the Regulation of the Mass Media: A Critical Review and Assessment," 52 N.C. L. Rev. 1, 70–71 (1973); Kalven, "Broadcasting, Public Policy and the First Amendment," 10 J. Law & Econ. 15, 19–23 (1967); Robinson, "The FCC and the First Amendment: Observations on 40 Years of Radio and Television Regulation," 52 Minn. L. Rev. 67, 136–40 (1967). The Supreme Court in *Red Lion* dismissed the broadcaster's chilling effect argument as speculative, while in *Miami Herald* it relied on the argument in striking down the regulation.

10. *New York Times Co. v. Sullivan*, 376 U.S. 254, 270 (1964).

11. See, e.g., 2 Z. Chaffee, *Government and Mass Communications* (Chicago: University of Chicago Press, 1947), 476–77.

12. One of the impeachment charges leveled by the House Judiciary Committee was that officials in the Nixon administration had induced, or had suggested inducing, tax audits of troublesome members of the media. See Congressional Information Service (1974), H521-34, at 16, 18, 21.

The willingness of the administration to employ federal machinery to silence the press was most vividly reflected in the events surrounding the creation of the "enemy list." John Dean, then the president's legal counsel, stated in one memorandum: "This memorandum addresses the matter of how we can maximize the fact of our incumbency in dealing with persons known to be active in their opposition to our administration. Stated a bit more bluntly—how can we use the available federal machinery to screw our political enemies." Congressional Information Service (1973), S961-64, at 1689. Dean went on to suggest that "grant availability, federal contracts, litigation, prosecution, etc." should all be considered in determining how most effectively to "screw" opponents. Id. The enemy list contained a total of fifty-six reporters, editors, columnists, and television commentators. Id. at 1716–18. The Washington Post, the New York Times, and the St. Louis Post Dispatch were among the institutions included. Id. at 1716. See also Washington Post, 3 December 1973 (documents disclosed by Senator

Lowell Weicker); *The White House Transcripts* (New York: Bantam, 1974), 57–58, 63, 404, 782–84. (See also n.51, infra, and accompanying text.)

13. In January 1973, the Associated Press and United Press International reported that the broadcast licenses of two Florida television stations, both owned by the Washington Post, were being challenged before the Federal Communications Commission by a group that included long-time friends and political associates of President Nixon. New York Times, 4 January 1973; Washington Post, 3 January 1973. It was subsequently revealed that Glenn J. Sedam, Jr., general counsel to the Committee for the Re-Election of the President, had advised some of the Nixon associates involved in the challenges. Washington Post, 9 January 1973. Only the Post's two stations, out of thirty-six stations in Florida, had their licenses contested. It should be noted, however, that the administration and all the principals involved in the challenges denied any political motivation. Washington Post, 9 January 1973. (See also n.51, infra, and accompanying text.)

14. Such data have been available with respect to broadcast regulation. We know, e.g., that in fiscal 1973 the commission received about 2,400 fairness doctrine complaints and forwarded ninety-four to broadcasters for comment. 39 Fed. Reg. 26,375 (1974).

15. For an indication that consideration of the type of person likely to assume the administrative role is relevant here, see *Times Film Corp. v. Chicago,* 365 U.S. 43, 69–73 (1961) (Chief Justice Warren dissenting). See also J. Milton, *Areopagitica* 210 (3 Harvard Classics [1909]).

16. As one commentator has argued: "Any widespread governmental action is likely to produce unexpected results. England, early in the eighteenth century, sought to strengthen her longstanding alliance with Portugal by admitting Portuguese wines at a very low rate of duty. This encouraged the drinking of port rather than French claret. The result was to afflict two centuries of Englishmen with gout. . . . Similar surprises can take place when the government concerns itself with communications industries." Z. Chafee, *Government and Mass Communications,* at 475. Perhaps an example of an unforeseen effect of broadcast regulation is the apparent political abuse surrounding the fairness doctrine. See F. Friendly, "What's Fair on the Air?" New York Times Magazine, 30 March 1975, at 11. Professor Friendly charges, inter alia, that during the early 1960s

officers of the Democratic National Committee organized and funded "private" organizations that would demand of radio and television stations an opportunity to reply to any coverage of right-wing positions in order to discourage media coverage of anti-administration viewpoints. (See also ch. 4, pp. 68–69, and n.48, infra, and accompanying text.)

17. Z. Chafee, supra, n.11, at 699–700.

18. Cf. E. Epstein, *News from Nowhere: TV and News* (New York: Random House, 1973), 150.

19. It is also likely that the principles represented by the regulations themselves have an effect throughout the entire media system. Representing the public's pronouncement of proper journalistic behavior, the principles may over time filter into the unregulated sphere, in much the same way that we occasionally see the constitutional due process requirements voluntarily adopted by private institutions. Thus, under a partial regulatory system, a fruitful symbiotic relationship may develop. (See also ch. 5, supra.)

20. The process resembles that which is observed in other areas of constitutional law, e.g., the applicability of criminal procedure rules to the juvenile justice system. Cf. *In re Winship,* 397 U.S. 358 (1970); *In re Gault,* 387 U.S. 1 (1967).

21. Z. Chafee, supra, n.11, at 11–12; Id. at 476–77; Kalven, supra n.9, at 18, 19–20. The only area, it seems, where the commission can perhaps be charged with having seriously ignored important free speech interests is that of indecent speech. See, e.g., *F.C.C. v. Pacifica Foundation,* 438 U.S. 726 (1978); *In re Pacifica Foundation,* 36 F.C.C. 147 (1964); *In re WUHY-FM Eastern Educ. Radio,* 24 F.C.C.2d 408 (1970). See Kalven, supra, n.9, at 18. (See also nn.48–62, infra, and accompanying text.)

22. See, e.g., *Columbia Broadcasting System, Inc. v. Democratic National Committee,* 412 U.S. 94 (1973); *National Broadcasting Co. v. FCC,* 516 F.2d 1101 (D.C. Cir. 1974), cert. denied, 424 U.S. 910 (1976).

23. Kalven, supra, n.9, at 38.

24. Id.

25. Id. at 37.

26. See Barron, "Access to the Press—a New First Amendment Right," 80 Harv. L. Rev. 1641 (1967); Barron, "An Emerging First Amendment Right of Access to the Media?" 37 Geo. Wash. L.

Rev. 487 (1969); Barron, "Access—the Only Choice for the Media?," 48 Tex. L. Rev. 766 (1970). Other articles on access are collected in Lange, supra. n.9, at 2 n.5.

The movement for a First Amendment right of access to the broadcast media was arrested by the Court's decision in *Columbia Broadcasting System, Inc. v. Democratic National Committee*, 412 U.S. 94 (1973).

27. Commission on Freedom of the Press, *A Free and Responsible Press* (Chicago: University of Chicago Press 1947), 25.

28. See generally M. McLuhan, *Understanding Media* (New York: McGraw-Hill, 1964); R. Williams, *Television: Technology and Cultural Form* (London: Fontana, 1974).

29. Professor Matthew Spitzer raises this potential criticism in his book, *Seven Dirty Words and Six Other Stories: Controlling the Content of Print and Broadcast* (New Haven: Yale University Press, 1986), 50. ("Partial Regulation provides much less protection against governmental tampering with the media than it otherwise might because more and more frequently one company owns broadcasting stations, newspapers, and magazines. This allows the government to punish a broadcasting station's parent corporation for misbehavior by its unregulated subsidiary.") Spitzer cites the example of the Watergate episode in which the Nixon White House attempted to pressure the Washington Post into abandoning its investigation. I also noted this in 1976 (see nn. 12 and 13, supra). This episode is described in greater detail in L. Powe, *American Broadcasting and the First Amendment* (Berkeley: University of California Press 1987), 121–41.

On the matter of cross-ownership, see generally Walter Baer, Henry Geller, Joseph Grundfest, and Karen Possner, "Concentration of Mass Media Ownership: Assessing the State of Current Knowledge," *Rand Corporation Report* (1974), 63; and William Gormley, Jr., *The Effects of Newspaper-Television Cross-Ownership on News Homogeneity* (Chapel Hill, N.C.: Institute for Research in Social Science, 1976), 19, 249–58.

30. See, e.g., I. Pool, *Technologies of Freedom* (Cambridge, Mass.: Harvard University Press, 1983), 39–42, 233–34.

31. See M. Spitzer, *Seven Dirty Words and Six Other Stories*, at 46–47: "Assuming that regulation effectively enhances access and diversity, Bollinger's concerns about these goals still do not suggest

regulating one of the media and not the other. By regulating all broadcasters but not all printed publications, the current system skews the distribution of values served in favor of those people who strongly prefer receiving one medium or the other. For example, those who cannot read, and who therefore strongly prefer broadcast, will be confined to the values of fair but homogenized communication. Conversely, those who live in areas unserved by broadcast may be confined to interesting but biased publications because none are subject to the fairness doctrine. Because millions of people cannot read and many own no television set, these effects are very important."

Spitzer goes on to speculate that a partial regulation approach "would suggest creating two classes of broadcasters and print publishers. Every geographic area of the country would have some licensed newspapers, subject to content controls, and some unlicensed newspapers, free from controls. Broadcasters would be similarly divided. In this fashion, those who cannot read would be exposed to the full panoply of first amendment values, as would those who live in areas unserved by broadcast." Id. at 47. This would require, he says, a system of subsidies of the regulated media. Spitzer concludes that common carrier regulation applied equally in both the broadcast and print media is in the end preferable.

Spitzer's concern about the futility of partial regulation in the absence of crossover audience is important, but more empirical data must be gathered before we can say how significant it is. Two additional points should be borne in mind. First, it is important to recognize that, even when there is no crossover, viewpoints and ideas entering by virtue of partial regulation may still spread generally throughout the marketplace of ideas. Second, to the extent that the absence of crossover constitutes a limitation on the achievements of such a regulatory scheme, it is still only a cost to be weighed in the ultimate comparison of all possible alternatives.

32. Federal Communications Commission, "General Fairness Doctrine Obligations of Broadcast Licensees," 50 FR 35418, 30 August 1985.

33. Krattenmaker and Powe, "The Fairness Doctrine Today: A Constitutional Curiosity and an Impossible Dream," 85 Duke L. J. 151 (1985).

34. See ch. 4, supra.

35. Id.

36. Z. Chafee, *Government and Mass Communications* (Chicago: University of Chicago Press, 1947), 680.

37. Id.

38. Id. at 689–99.

39. Id. at 699–700.

40. Id. at 702–19.

41. Federal Communications Commission, *General Fairness Doctrine Obligations of Broadcast Licensees,* 102 F.C.C.2d 143 (1985), para. 63, p. 185 (which mentions that the NAD provided the commission with "45 examples of the way in which the fairness doctrine chills broadcasters' speech," many of which are individually noted throughout the report), para. 32, pp. 163–64 ("Since broadcast time is a valuable resource, such a requirement imposes costs upon the licensee. In order to avoid these costs, a broadcaster may be inhibited from presenting more than a minimal amount of controversial issue programming"), para. 33, p. 164 ("A licensee may also be inhibited from presenting controversial issue programming by the fear of incurring the various expenses and other burdens which may arise in the context of fairness doctrine litigation"), and para. 35, p. 165 ("Broadcasters can also be deterred by the financial costs involved in defending a fairness doctrine complaint").

42. Federal Communications Commission, *General Fairness Doctrine Obligations of Broadcast Licensees,* 102 F.C.C.2d 143 (1985), para. 58, p. 181.

43. Id. at para. 29, p. 161, n.66.

44. *Red Lion* at 392–95.

45. The reluctance of the commissioners to enforce the first part of the fairness doctrine is expressed by FCC Commissioner Glen O. Robinson's statement that "concededly, enforcement of the first obligation constitutes a somewhat greater degree of government interference than enforcement of the second inasmuch as it is not triggered by the *licensee's* program choice." Representative Patsy Mink, 59 F.C.C.2d 987, 99 at n.1 (1976) (concurring statement). Though this view has been commonly expressed, it has never been explained to my satisfaction why telling broadcasters what issues should be discussed involves a "greater degree of government interference" than telling broadcasters what viewpoints should be discussed.

46. 412 U.S. 94 (1973). See also chap. 4, supra.

47. In 1855, 150,000 people gathered in the northeast corner of London's Hyde Park to demonstrate against the Sunday Trading Bill. At that time, there was no legal right of assembly in the park, and police came to arrest any inflammatory orator. After more demonstrations, the right of assembly was recognized in 1872, and that part of the park became known as the Speaker's Corner. Ben Weinreb and Christopher Hibbert, eds., *The London Encyclopedia* (London: Macmillan, 1983), 402.

48. L. Powe, *American Broadcasting and the First Amendment* (Berkeley: University of California Press, 1987).

49. See n.21, supra, and accompanying text. See also n.34 in ch. 5, supra.

50. Powe, *American Broadcasting,* at 248.

51. Id. at 13–30. See *Trinity Methodist Church v. F.R.C.,* 62 F.2d 850 (D.C.C.R. 1932).

52. Id. at 112–17.

53. Id. at ch. 10.

54. Id. at ch. 5.

55. Id. at ch. 8.

56. Id. at ch. 9.

57. Id. at 254–55.

58. See, e.g., *F.C.C. v. National Citizens Committee for Broadcasting,* 436 U.S. 775 (1978).

59. Powe, *American Broadcasting,* at 132.

60. Id., at 137–41.

61. See, e.g., *F.C.C. v. Pacifica Foundation,* 438 U.S. 726 (1978).

62. See *Office of Communication of United Church of Christ v. F.C.C.,* 425 F.2d 543 (D.C. Cir. 1969).

CHAPTER SEVEN

1. 1967 U.S. Code Congressional & Administrative News 1772–75.

2. See Federal Communications Commission, General Fairness Doctrine Obligations of Broadcast Licensees, 102 F.C.C.2d 143 (1985).

3. See, e.g., M. Spitzer, *Seven Dirty Words and Six Other Sto-*

ries: Controlling the Content of Print and Broadcast (New Haven: Yale University Press, 1986).

4. See ch. 6, pp. 110–11, and nn. 2–7 therein.

5. Owen M. Fiss, "Why the State?" 100 Harv. L. Rev. 781 (1987).

6. Id. at 781, 788. See R. Williams, *Communications,* 3d ed. (New York: Penguin, 1976), 108–9, 32–33.

7. The closest the Supreme Court has come to acknowledging any problems was in *Federal Communications Commission v. League of Women Voters,* 468 U.S. 364 (1984): "The prevailing rationale for broadcast regulation based on spectrum scarcity has come under increasing criticism in recent years. Critics, including the incumbent Chairman of the F.C.C., charge that with the advent of cable and satellite television technology, communities now have access to such a wide variety of stations that the scarcity doctrine is obsolete. . . . We are not prepared, however, to reconsider our longstanding approach without some signal from Congress or the F.C.C. that technological developments have advanced so far that some revision of the system of broadcast regulation may be required." Id., at 376 n.11. The most recent Supreme Court decision relies on the reasoning of *Red Lion.* See *Metro Broadcasting, Inc. v. F.C.C.,* 110 S. Ct. 2997, 3010–11 (1990).

Lower courts have been more forthrightly critical. See *Syracuse Peace Council v. Federal Communications Commission,* 867 F.2d 654 (D.C. Cir. 1989), *cert. denied,* 110 Sup. Ct. 717 (1990); *Telecommunications Research & Action Center v. Federal Communications Commission,* 801 F.2d 501 (D.C. Cir. 1986), *cert. denied,* 482 U.S. 919 (1987).

8. See Note, "Cable Television and the First Amendment," 71 Colum. L. Rev. 1008 (1971).

9. See I. Pool, *Technologies of Freedom* (Cambridge, Mass.: Harvard University Press, 1983), 166–76. But see G. Shapiro, P. Kurland, and J. Mercurio, *"Cablespeech": The Case for First Amendment Protection* (New York: Harcourt Brace Jovanovich, 1983), 1013.

10. See, generally, Sunstein, "Legal Interference with Private Preferences," 53 U. Chicago L. Rev. 1129 (1986). See also R. Williams, *Communications,* at 129–37.

11. *Pell v. Procunier,* 417 U.S. 817 (1974); *Saxbe v. Washington*

Post Co., 417 U.S. 843 (1974); *Houchins v. KQED,* 438 U.S. 1 (1978).

12. *Gannett Co. v. DePasquale,* 443 U.S. 368 (1979).

13. *Richmond Newspapers, Inc. v. Virginia,* 448 U.S. 555.

14. See *Branzburg v. Hayes,* 408 U.S. 665, 684 (1972).

15. *United States v. The Progressive, Inc.,* 467 F.Supp. 990 (W.D. Wisc. 1979).

16. See Alexander Bickel, *The Morality of Consent* (New Haven: Yale University Press, 1975), 78–86.

The government is entitled to keep things private and will attain as much privacy as it can get away with politically by guarding its privacy internally. . . . Yet the power to arrange security at the source, looked at in itself, is great, and if it were nowhere countervailed it would be quite frightening—is anyway, perhaps—since the law in no wise guarantees its prudent exercise or even effectively guards against its abuse. But there *is* countervailing power. The press, by which is meant anybody, not only the institutionalized print and electronic press, can be prevented from publishing only in extreme and quite dire circumstances. . . . It is a disorderly situation surely. But if we ordered it we would have to sacrifice one of two contending values—privacy or public disclosure—which are ultimately irreconcilable. If we should let the government censor as well as withhold, that would be too much dangerous power, and too much privacy. If we should allow the government neither to censor nor withhold, that would provide far too little privacy of decision-making and too much power in the press and in Congress. (Bickel, *Morality of Consent,* at 79–80; emphasis in original)

17. *State v. Lashinsky,* 81 N.J. 1, 404 A.2d 1121 (1979).

18. The New Jersey Supreme Court upheld Lashinsky's conviction, and a $15 fine, but seemed to leave the constitutional door ajar by cautioning that the press cannot be completely excluded from newsworthy events.

19. The point is made in greater depth in S. Bok, *Secrets: On the Ethics of Concealment and Revelation* (New York: Vintage, 1984), 26–27.

Broadcast regulation, *continued*
as restrained by the
autonomy principle, 97,
114–16, 153; scarcity
rationale for, 67–73,
88–90, 93–97, 101
Burger, Warren, 103

Cable television regulation,
99, 134, 136, 143–144
Carnegie Commission on
Educational Television,
report of, 107
Central image, concept of,
1–2, 20, 23, 25, 31, 44, 50,
108, 123, 133, 139, 145,
151
Chafee, Zechariah, 28, 91,
110, 124–25, 162n.5,
185n.14, 193n.2, 195n.11,
196n.16, 196n.17, 197n.21,
199n.36
Chain broadcasting. *See*
Broadcast regulation
Choper, Jesse, 185n.21
Coase, Ronald, 93, 186n.25
*Columbia Broadcasting System,
Inc. v. Democratic National
Committee,* 70, 92, 98, 104,
115, 127
*Columbia Broadcasting System,
Inc. v. FCC,* 71, 96
Commission on Freedom of
the Press. *See* Hutchins
Commission on Freedom
of the Press
Communications Act of 1934.
See Broadcast regulation
Concentration of ownership in
the media, 27, 29–30,
37–38, 53–54, 93–95,

109–20, 134, 136–41,
144
*Cox Broadcasting Corp. v.
Cohn,* 12, 26, 35, 36

Defamation. *See* Freedom of
the press; Libel
Denniston, Lyle, 174n.28,
178n.44
Distortion of news, regulation
of. *See* Broadcast regulation
Douglas, William O., 91, 103,
121, 185n.17
Dworkin, Ronald, 178n.45,
178n.49

Electronic media. *See*
Broadcast regulation; Cable
television regulation
Emerson, Thomas, 91,
171n.22, 175n.28, 185n.19,
186n.27, 193n.3
Epstein, Edward, 196n.18
Equal time rule. *See* Broadcast
regulation

Fairness doctrine. *See*
Broadcast regulation
Fair trial, free press. *See*
Freedom of the press
Falwell, Jerry, 14–15
FCC v. Midwest Video Corp.
(II), 104, 105, 106
Federal Communications
Commission. *See* Broadcast
regulation; Cable television
regulation
Fiss, Owen, 137, 142, 184n.2,
201n.5
Florida Star v. B. J. F., 13, 26
Format, regulation of. *See*
Broadcast regulation

Fowler, Mark, 184n.1
Frankfurter, Felix, 67, 88
Franklin, Marc. 170n.21
A Free and Responsible Press,
report of the Hutchins
Commission. *See* Hutchins
Commission
Freedom of the press, the
costs to public debate,
26–39; and fair trial, 16–17;
intentional infliction of
emotional distress, 14–15;
libel (defamation), 2–10,
25–26, 35–36, 43–46, 50,
91, 123, 151, 154; national
security, 10–11, 48–49,
50–51, 147–48;
newsgathering right, 17–19,
58, 145–51, 154; prior
restraints, 10–11, 16–17,
48–49, 50–51; privacy,
invasion of, 12–14, 35–37,
46, 139, 151; reporter's
privilege, 18–19, 20, 54,
58; taxation of the press,
15–16; undervaluation of
the costs of, 24–26, 38–39.
See also Broadcast
regulation; Cable television
regulation; Concentration
of ownership in the media;
Public broadcasting; Public
regulation of the press,
theory of.
Friendly, Fred, 68–69, 129,
167n.40, 182n.19, 196n.16

Gertz v. Robert Welch, Inc., 9,
10, 45
*Globe Newspaper Co. v.
Superior Court*, 17

Goldstein, Tom, 177n.39,
178n.48
Goodale, James, 170n.21
Goodman, Walter, 177n.40
Goodwin, H. Eugene,
178n.48
Gunther, Gerald, 185n.20

Henry, William, 167n.40
*Hustler Magazine, Inc. v.
Falwell*, 14
Hutchins, Robert, 28,
186n.22
Hutchins Commission Report
on Freedom of the Press,
27–34, 40, 54, 59, 60, 91,
92, 97, 107, 118, 124–25,
135, 145, 154
Hutchinson v. Proxmire, 10
Hyde Park Corner, 128

Indecent programming. *See*
Broadcast regulation
Intentional inflictions of
emotional distress. *See*
Freedom of the press

Journalistic autonomy,
principle of, 1–39. *See also*
Central image, concept of;
Freedom of the press

Kalven, Harry, 7–8, 51, 81,
91, 115, 145, 150, 154,
157n.3, 158n.13, 172n.24,
184n.12, 187n.34, 194n.7,
195n.9, 197n.21, 197n.23
Kamisar, Yale, 185n.21
Katz, Steven, 170n.20
Krattenmaker, Thomas,
184n.1, 199n.33
Kurland, Philip, 202n.9